Table of Contents

Chapter 1
Algebra

What is algebra?

Algebra is the use of letters and symbols to represent numbers and values to describe relationships

I play with my kids called "Agent X". Here is how it works, I write something down and you have to tell me the secret identity of Agent X.

Case 1: $X + 4 = 7$
Who is Agent X?

Sure this is a ploy used to masquerade algebra as a game. The X in this case is a letter that represents a specific number that describes the relationship between 4 and 7. In case you can't figure it out, Agent X is 3.

Who is Agent X?

Consider another example. You are writing a book and you participate in a writing group. You may call these your α (alpha) readers. α is a Greek letter that represents a person and describes their relationship to you and your writing process. It might be a stretch, but I would call that algebra.

In 8th grade we would ask Mr. Anderson, "When will we ever use algebra in our lives?" The answer is simple, there are opportunities to use it every day.

The objective of this chapter is to learn basic algebraic principles and how they apply to business settings.

Linear equations is a fancy way to say straight lines. We can write out an equation that represents a straight line. The standard form of a linear equation is

$$ax + by = c$$

Here, x and y are the variables. Variables are letters that represent unknown numbers or values. The letters a, b, and c are parameters and represent known numbers.

Example 1.1a: $3x + 5y = 15$

In this example, we plugged in known numbers for a, b, and c but we still don't know what x and y are. If I were to plug in a number for x, there is only one value for y. Consider if $x = 0$, then $y = 3$. If $x = 1$, then $y = \frac{12}{5}$ or 2.4.

These couplets, or pairs and x and y, fall along a straight line. This is why we call this a linear equation (linear = straight line).

Example 1.1b: $4x - 2y = 12$ if $x = 2$ solve for y.

Solution Example 1.1b:

$$4(2) - 2y = 12 \qquad \text{Plug 2 into x}$$
$$8 - 2y = 12 \qquad \text{Subtract 8 from each side}$$
$$-2y = 4 \qquad \text{Divide each side by -2}$$
$$y = -2 \qquad \text{Final Answer}$$

I am confident that you have the ability to solve a simple equation like $8 - 2y = 12$, but just in case you don't have the same confidence in yourself, you can use Excel to solve this type of equation and check your work.

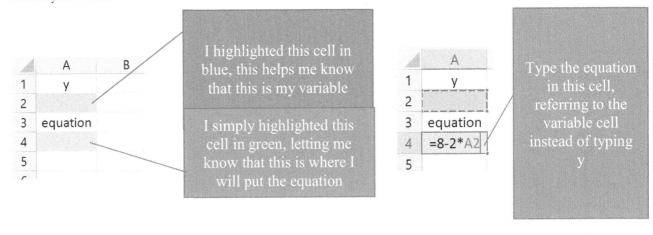

	A	B
1	y	
2		
3	equation	
4		
5		

I highlighted this cell in blue, this helps me know that this is my variable

I simply highlighted this cell in green, letting me know that this is where I will put the equation

	A
1	y
2	
3	equation
4	=8-2*A2
5	

Type the equation in this cell, referring to the variable cell instead of typing y

Go to the Data tab in the ribbon and click on the What-If Analysis

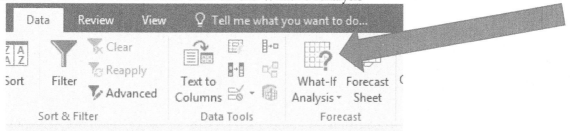

Click on Goal Seek and fill in the values according to the formula

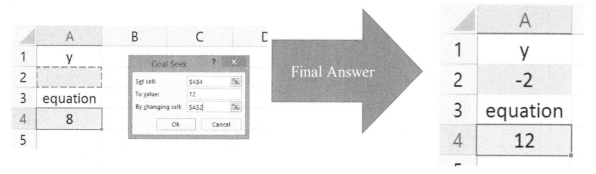

YouTube Video on Goal Seek: https://youtu.be/qoGmWOtlvZA

Goal Seek is a powerful tool that excel has that can help solve algebraic equations, especially linear equations.

Example 1.1.c Using Goal Seek, solve the following equations

(i) $4x + 5 = 21$

(ii) $-4x + 5 = 21$

(iii) $.52 - .21x = 4.3$

Solutions Example 1.1c

(i)	$x = 4$
(ii)	$x = -4$
(iii)	$x = -18$

Note: It is really important that you work the example problems in the textbook out on your own. Seeing the correct answer is not the purpose of studying, learning how to work the problem on your own is the key. Make sure you do this!!!!

Chapter 1.2 Graphing Linear Equations

As we have worked on linear equations, you might say to yourself, but I learned to write straight lines with the following equation:

$$y = mx + b$$

That's right, I also learned this equation (Mr. Anderson was a pretty good math teacher). This equation is just the standard linear equation written out solved for y.

Example 1.2a Given $ax + by = c$, solve for y

Solution Example 1.2a

$ax + by = c$	Subtract ax from each side
$by = c - ax$	Divide each side by b
$y = \frac{c}{b} - \frac{a}{b}x$	Relabel parameters
$let \frac{c}{b} = b \qquad Let -\frac{a}{b} = m$	
$y = b + mx$	Reorder the terms
$y = mx + b$	Final Answer

Writing the equation this way is called the slope-intercept form. This is because m represents the slope of the line and b is the y-intercept. This is really useful when you want to represent the equation on a graph.

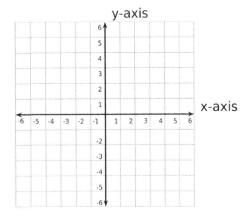

The official term of this type of graph is the Cartesian plane. Trust me when I say that you can impress people at a party by talking about the Cartesian plane. A good conversation starter is to ask someone their favorite quadrant, but we digress.

The Cartesian plane shows a grid with y on the vertical axis and x on the horizontal axis.

Example 1.2b Graph out the equation $y = 1x + 1$

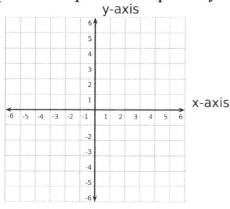

Solution Example 1.2b

Let's identify the key points. In this case, $b = 1$ which means that the y-intercept is 1. This is the value of y when $x = 0$. Don't believe me? Plug in 0 for x and you will get $y = 1$

The slope of the line is $m = 1$. This means for every time you add one to x, you have to add one to y.

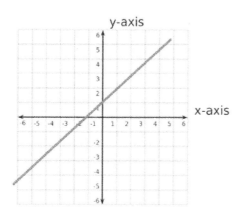

The red line is the graphically representation of $y = 1x + 1$

Let's talk about some important characteristics of the slope (m) and the y-intercept (b)

Slope

- Slope of the line: $m = \dfrac{rise}{run} = \dfrac{\Delta y}{\Delta x}$

- Note: The Greek symbol Δ means change or difference. So $\dfrac{\Delta y}{\Delta x}$ is read, the change in y for a change in x

- Given two points, the slope can be calculated with the following equation: $m = \dfrac{y_2 - y_1}{x_2 - x_1}$

- For a vertical line, $\Delta x = 0$. Since bad things happen when you divide by zero, the slope of the vertical line is undefined. (one way to think about that is that the slope is infinity)
- For a horizontal line, $\Delta y = 0$. Bad things don't happen when the numerator is zero, so the slope is 0.

Intercept
- Generally, the intercept is where the line crosses an axis.
- The y-intercept is where the line crosses the y-axis
- The y-intercept can be found with the slope-intercept form, b
- The y-intercept can also be found by plugging $x = 0$ and solve for y
- The x-intercept is where the line crosses the x-axis
- The y-intercept can be found by plugging $y = 0$ and solve for x

How about you talk now. Find someone else and explain to them the answer to these questions
  (i)   What is the interpretation of the slope?
  (ii)   What does the slope tell you?
  (iii)   What is the interpretation of the y-intercept?

Example 1.2c Find the equation of the line that passes through the points (5, 8) and (7, 14)

Example 1.2d Find the *y*-intercept of $5x + y = 9$

Example 1.2e Find the *x*-intercept of $y = 9x - 72$

Note: If you do not know how to type mathematical equations in Word, you need to learn how to do this. One was is to insert an Equation. To do this, in the ribbon Insert>Equation. The shortcut to insert an equation is to hold ALT and then type =.
See video: https://youtu.be/16n-pb8iypA
                    https://youtu.be/VNGQCPMg62w

Solution Example 1.2c Find the equation of the line that passes through the points (5, 8) and (7, 14)

$$slope = \frac{\Delta y}{\Delta x} = \frac{14-8}{7-5} = 3$$
To find intercept: $y = 3x + b$
Plug in any point
$8 = 3(5) + b$
$b = -7$
$y = 3x - 7$

Example 1.2d Find the y-intercept of $5x + y = 9$

Set $x = 0$, solve for y, $y = 9$

Example 1.2e Find the x-intercept of $y = 9x - 72$

Set $y = 0, 0 = 9x - 72$
$72 = 9x$
$x = 8$

Excel can be used to graph out linear equations. Consider the following equation:
$$y = -3x + 7$$

In Excel, we want to set up two columns, one that has potential x values and the other that will give the value of y given the x value. Let's start first with the column for x's.

	A	B
1	x	y = -3x + 7
2		-10
3		-9
4		-8
5		-7
6		-6
7		-5
8		-4
9		-3
10		-2
11		-1
12		0
13		1
14		2
15		3
16		4
17		5
18		6
19		7
20		8
21		9
22		10

For this graph, let's go from -10 to 10

Shortcut: type first two values, highlight them, click lower right corner and drag the box down

	A	B
1	x	y = -3x + 7
2		-10 =-3*A2+7
3		-9
4		0

Type in the equation into cell B2 referencing cell A2

	A	B
1	x	y = -3x + 7
2		-10 37
3		-9

Shortcut: to copy and paste all the way down, double click the box on the lower right corner

9

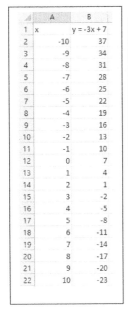

	A	B
1	x	y = -3x + 7
2	-10	37
3	-9	34
4	-8	31
5	-7	28
6	-6	25
7	-5	22
8	-4	19
9	-3	16
10	-2	13
11	-1	10
12	0	7
13	1	4
14	2	1
15	3	-2
16	4	-5
17	5	-8
18	6	-11
19	7	-14
20	8	-17
21	9	-20
22	10	-23

Now that we have the values, let's start creating a line chart

Creating a Line Chart

In the ribbon, go to Insert then click on Line Chart

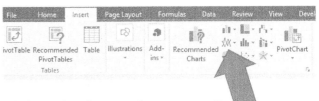

Click on the chart on the top row, fou[r] [o]ne over (Line with Markers)

This should create a blank white box in the middle of your worksheet. Right click on the box and click on Select Data.

In the Legend Entries (Series) box, click on Add, then you can add a series name by hand or click on cell B2. Then for Series values, highlight cells B2 to B22, or the values for the equation.

This should insert a line into the graph. It is looking better but notice that the x-values do not line up. It starts at 1 and goes to 21 when our values should go from -10 to 10.

In the Horizontal (Category) Axis Labels, click Edit. Highlight the values of x from cells A2 to A22.

Click OK and presto change-o, you just graphed the equation.
     YouTube Video on graphing a linear equation: https://youtu.be/3UHHQGzkvE8

Suppose now that instead of the equation $y = -3x + 7$ we want to graph the equation $y = -3x + 8$? To do this, we would have to click on the cell B2 and change the equation. Then copy and paste it down. Each time the equation changes, you would have to follow the same process.

Instead, we could set up the spreadsheet and parameterize the equation. Sounds technical and it may be, but it really allows you to create awesome spreadsheets. Using parameters allows you to do what is called spreadsheet modeling, and it is totally in vogue these days.

What is a parameter? A parameter is a non-variable value in a function, in this case it is m and b (slope and y-intercept). Let's look at an equation to highlight how to do this.

Consider $y = 4x + 2$

In this case, the slope is 4 and the y-intercept is 2. This comes directly from the slope intercept form, $y = mx + b$. In this equation, the letters m and b are parameters. They represent known numbers. In our case, they represent 4 and 2, respectively.

To parameterize, we would set up a new worksheet in Excel, and create a cell for parameters m and b. We then would set up a column for x and y, similar to what we did before. For the equation, we don't type in 4 and 2, but reference the cell for m (A2) and the cell for b (B2). See below:

	A	B	C
1	m	b	
2			
3	x	y	
4		0	=$A$2*A4+$B$2
5		1	

What are those dollar signs? These are called anchors, and anchor the reference to that specific cell. As you copy and paste, Excel draws upon cells with reference to the original cell. That is why it draws upon the cell to the left as we copy and paste the function down the row. But when referring to m and b, we want it to always refer to these exact cells. So as you can type $A$2 by hand or click on the A2 cell and then hit F4. That will automatically add the anchors.

Once you do this, copy and paste the function all the way down. Then put in 4 and 2 into the parameter cells. You can create the graph the same way as before, or you can skip a step by highlighting the y values then insert chart > Line with Markers. This will add the series for you automatically, you will still need to right click and edit the horizontal axis.

Once you have this graph set up, it is easy to graph other linear equations. Want to graph out $y = 2x + 4$? No problem just type in 2 and 4 into their respective cells. it will automatically adjust your graph.

Chapter 1.3 Application: Demand Curve

For this application we want to apply what we have learned to a specific setting seen in business. This application is about the demand curve.

When producing a product, what are the factors that affect the sales of the product?
There are a lot factors: price of your product, price of the competitors product, advertising, size of the market, income of the target consumer, and so on. We can take all these factors and write a real complicated relationship between each factor and the number of sales. We will save that for another day, even another class.

Let's just focus on one thing that is in your control, the price you charge for you product. You can now write an equation to represent the relationship between the price you charge and the number of sales. Instead of using x and y, let's use other letters to represent sales (Q for quantity) and price (P for price).

We will talk later in this class (Regression Section) how to calculate a demand curve, but let's assume the following demand curve for your business.

$$Q = 150 - 2P$$

Given this equation, what does the slope of the demand equation tell us?

Remember back to the generic interpretation of the slope; that is the change in y for a change in x. In this case, we just substitute in the terms quantity and price wherever we see x and y.

Therefore, the slope of the demand equation tells us the change in quantity for a change in price. In other words, and possibly more intuitive, it describes the relationship between the price of the good and the amount that the consumers will demand.

For our example, the slope is -2. That is to say then, that for each dollar increase in price the demand will decrease by 2. It is also the case that if the price were to decrease by a dollar then the quantity demanded will increase by 2.

> Note: The demand equation is written as quantity as a function of price. That is, quantity is the y variable and price is the x variable.

Inverse Demand Equation

When graphing demand equations, they are usually graphed with P on the vertical axis, as the dependent variable and Q as the variable on the right hand side of the equation. When the demand equation is rearranged so that P is the dependent variable, it is called an *inverse demand equation*.

Example 1.3a take the demand equation: Q = 150 – 2P and rewrite it as the inverse demand equation.

Solution Example 1.3a

$Q = 150 - 2P$	Subtract 15 from each side
$Q - 150 = -2P$	Divide each side by -2
$-\frac{1}{2}Q + 75 = P$	Reorder terms
$P = 75 - \frac{1}{2}Q$	Final Answer

Example 1.3b Graph out the Inverse Demand Equation $P = 75 - \frac{1}{2}Q$ by hand

Price

Quantity

13

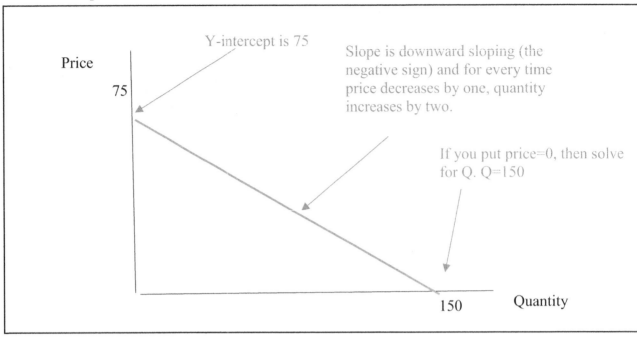

Price

75

Y-intercept is 75

Slope is downward sloping (the negative sign) and for every time price decreases by one, quantity increases by two.

If you put price=0, then solve for Q. Q=150

150   Quantity

Example 1.3c Graph the inverse demand equation: $Q = 7500 - 10P$

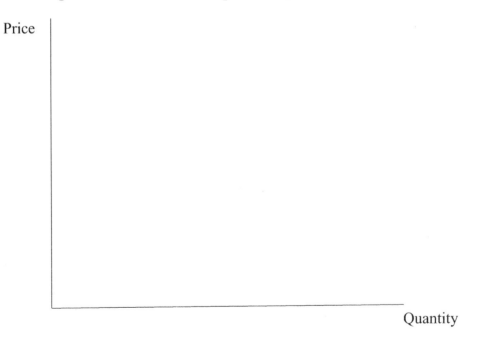

Price

Quantity

14

Solution Example 1.3c

Step 1, rewrite the demand equation and the inverse demand equation

$Q = 7500 - 10P$ ⠀⠀⠀⠀⠀⠀ Subtract 7500 from each side

$Q - 7500 = -10P$ ⠀⠀⠀⠀⠀ Divide each side by -10, reorder terms

$P = 750 - \frac{1}{10}Q$

Step 2, Graph out the inverse demand equation

Price

Y-intercept is 750

x-intercept is 7500, set P=0 and solve for Q

Quantity

Example 1.3d A firm has a demand equation represented by $Q = 150 - \frac{1}{4}P$

Write out the inverse demand equation

If the firm produces and sells exactly 200 units, what was the price that was charged?

The price is set at $200 and you produce 150 units. What is your inventory?

15

Write out the inverse demand equation

> Inverse Demand Equation $P = 600 - 4Q$

If the firm produces and sells exactly 200 units, what was the price that was charged?

> If the firm sells Q=200 $P = \$200$

The price is set at $200 and you produce 150 units. What is your inventory?

> If the price is set at $200 and you produce 150 unit, what is your inventory?
> At the price of $200, the Quantity would be 100. That is the quantity demanded by the consumers. Thus if you produce 150 units, you will have a surplus of 50, which is your inventory

Chapter 1.4 Application: Depreciation

This is an example of an application of the linear equation. The key is to remember that we can substitute any letters or symbols for x and y. What's in a variable? That which we call a rose by any other name would smell so sweet. Even Bill Shakespeare knew that you could substitute other letters into the traditional x,y format.

One of my first "real" jobs was working at a plant that made paper bags. The process was automated by some pretty large machines. These machines would take a giant roll of paper (8 feet tall) and run it through and spit out 500 paper grocery bags printed and packed ready for shipment.

The company, Weyerhauser, would buy these machines for several million dollars. If they could calculate depreciation, then they could amortize the costs of the purchase over the life of the machine. This is important because accountants can take that information and help you save millions of dollars in taxes.

Assuming depreciation is linear, can you draw a rough sketch of what depreciation might look like on a graph? Could you explain what your graph means to someone else? Then do so now.

Example 1.4a: The value of a firm's delivery truck (v) after t years has been estimated as $v = 65000 - 7500t$

What is the initial value?

What is its value after 4 years?

When is it worn out?

Draw it out on a graph.

Value

Time

Solution Example 1.4a

What is the initial cost?

This is the same as asking what the y-intercept is. The y-intercept is the value of y when x is zero. For this problem, we are asking, what is the value when time is zero, or what is the initial value? Therefore, set t=0 and you get v=65,000

What is its value after 4 years?

Set t=4 and then solve for v. $v(4) = 65,000 - 7,500(4) = 35,000$

When is it worn out?

This is asking when the value is equal to zero, or the value of the x-intercept. Therefore, set v=0, then solve for t. t=8.67, meaning that at time equals 8.67 the delivery truck has no value.

Draw it out on a graph.

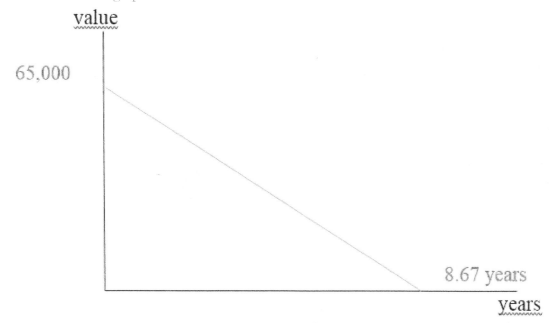

See Video: https://www.youtube.com/watch?v=ILcXozcjuZI

Chapter 1.5 Application: Break-Even Analysis

Break-even analysis can be seen as another application of the linear equation (later we will look at a break-even analysis using non-linear equations #foreshadowing). Break-even refers to the point when total revenue equals total cost, or when profits are zero. Producing slightly less will lead to a loss and producing slightly more will produce a small profit.

So it is important to review the definition of total revenues and profits. This is very important to know so I will just go ahead and highlight it for you, see the box below.

> Remember
> Total Revenue = Price x Quantity (TR = P x Q)
> Profits = Total Revenue – Total Cost (π = TR – TC)

Example 1.5a Consider the following equations which tells the relationship between the quantity produced (Q) by the firm and the Total Revenues earned (TR) and the Total Costs incurred (TC).

$$TR = 45Q \qquad TC = 560 + 9Q$$

What is fixed cost (FC) and variable cost (VC)?

What price is the firm charging?

What is profit when $Q = 100$?

What is fixed cost (FC) and variable cost (VC)?

FC is cost that is independent of Q, or in this case FC=560
VC is cost that depends on Q, in this case VC=9Q

What price is the firm charging?

TR=P*Q, so in this case, P=45

What is profit when $Q = 100$?

Profits$(\pi) = TR - TC$, in this case $\pi(100) = 45(100) - \left(560 + 9(100)\right) = 3040$

Example 1.5b What is the break-even point?

Solution Example 1.5a

Break-even point is when total revenue equals total cost
$$45Q = (560 + 9Q)$$
$$560 = 36Q$$
$$Q = 15.56$$
Another way to solve for break-even point is when profits = 0.
$$45(Q) - \left(560 + 9(Q)\right)=0$$
Solve for Q
$$Q = 15.56$$

Chapter 1.6 Quadratic Functions

A function is a rule that assigns each value of the variable x to one and only value of y. But instead of saying y, we say f of x or f(x). Whereas before we would write $y = 5x + 2$, now to rewrite that as a function you would write $f(x) = 5x + 2$. That's all there really is to it.

As for some important properties of a function see the following:
- The possible values of x are called the domain
- The resulting values of f(x) are called the range.
- A function assigns an x to one and only one value of f(x). This is often talked about with a vertical line test. If you draw a vertical line and it touches the function in more than one spot, it fails the test and is not a function.
- A single f(x) value can be derived from 2 different x values. For example, $f(x) = x^2$. The values of $x = -2$ and $x = 2$ both give the f(x) value of 4. This is still a function. No horizontal line test.
- Check out these two songs to help you learn more about functions
  - Function Rap
  - The Function Song

There are countless types of functions.
- Linear Function $f(x) = 4x + 5$
- Quadratic Function $f(x) = 2x^2 + 4x + 5$
- Cubic Function $f(x) = -2x^3 + 2x^2 + 4x + 5$
- Log Function $f(x) = \ln(x)$
- Exponential Function $f(x) = e^x$

We covered Linear Functions earlier in this chapter in sections 1.1 and 1.2. In this section, we want to focus on Quadratic Functions. Quadratic functions are parabolic in shape, that is they are curves in the shape of frowny and smiley faces.

A generic form of a quadratic function is
$$f(x) = ax^2 + bx + c.$$

Here a, b, and c are parameters that represents numbers. Consider the following examples
- $f(x) = 4x^2 - 2x - 7$ where $a = 4, b = -2, c = -7$
- $f(x) = 2x^2$ where $a = 2, b = 0, c = 0$

      You could even write the linear function as a special case of the quadratic
- $f(x) = 3x + 5$ where $a = 0, b = 3, c = 5$

Two of the more important parts of a quadratic function is where the function is equal to zero (the roots) and where the function reaches a minimum or maximum (the vertex). Consider briefly the following graph, show the relationship between profits (on the y-axis) and quantity produced on the x-axis.

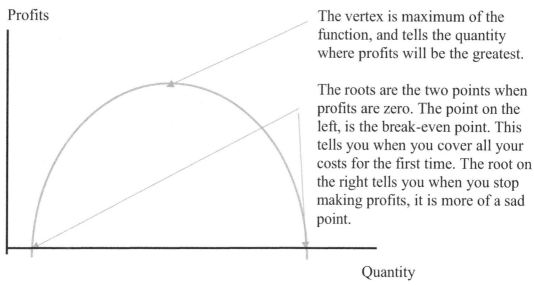

Profits

The vertex is maximum of the function, and tells the quantity where profits will be the greatest.

The roots are the two points when profits are zero. The point on the left, is the break-even point. This tells you when you cover all your costs for the first time. The root on the right tells you when you stop making profits, it is more of a sad point.

Quantity

Finding the roots

To find the roots, you need to solve the following generic equation:

$$ax^2 + bx + c = 0$$

Solving this equation will give up to two values of x where the function crosses the x-axis. There are multiple methods to solve this equation.

Method 1: Factoring

To solve by factoring you ask, what multiplies into $a * c$ and adds into b? It may be easier to see with an example.

$$f(x) = x^2 + 5x + 6 = 0$$

What multiplies into 6 but adds into 5? The answer is 3 and 2. Therefore, you can factor the function into the following:

$(x + 3)(x + 2) = 0$ (if you don't believe me, FOIL this out and see if you get the same function from above)

This equation is true when either expression in parenthesis is equals 0.
$(x + 3) = 0$ and $(x + 2) = 0$

Solve for x in each equation and you get the solution is
$x = -3$ and $x = -2$

Solving by factoring is nice when it is easy to saran wrap or factor a quadratic equation, but if the equation does not factor easily, then we might think of another method.

Method 2: Quadratic Formula

The quadratic formula gives the solution to quadratic equations (if a solution exists), or tells us where the x-intercepts are (where $f(x) = 0$):

> # QUADRATIC FORMULA
>
> $$x = \frac{-b \pm \sqrt{b^2 - 4ac}}{2a}$$

Note: the quadratic formula gives two solutions (or roots). One when you add the square root and one where you subtract the square root.
To help your remember this, check out the following jingle:
https://www.youtube.com/watch?v=2lbABbfU6Zc

You could also spend hours googling quadratic equation songs, there are a lot of really bad ones out there. All of which say exactly what we wrote in the box above.

Let's apply the quadratic formula to the following equation

$$f(x) = x^2 + 5x + 6 = 0$$

$$x_1 = \frac{-5 + \sqrt{5^2 - 4(1)(6)}}{2(1)} = \frac{-5 + \sqrt{1}}{2} = -2$$

$$x_2 = \frac{-5 - \sqrt{5^2 - 4(1)(6)}}{2(1)} = \frac{-5 - \sqrt{1}}{2} = -3$$

> Note: if you get a negative value inside the square root, this means that there are no real solutions, or that the function never crosses the x-axis. In that case, you would say that there is no solution.

Finding the Vertex
The other interesting point of a quadratic function is the vertex. This is the point where the function reaches a maximum or minimum value. Consider a graphical representation of two different quadratic functions.

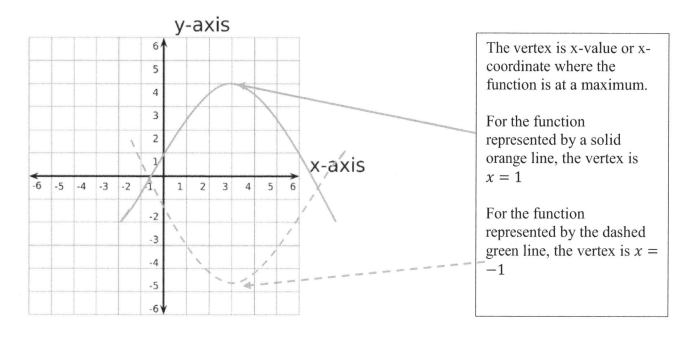

We can calculate the vertex, or the x-coordinate of the middle of the parabola with the following equation:

$$X\text{-COORDINATE OF THE VERTEX}$$
$$x = -\frac{b}{2a}$$

Consider the function $f(x) = -3x^2 - 3x + 6$, what is the x-coordinate of the vertex?

We just have to plug and chug with this equation.

$$x = -\frac{-3}{2(-3)} = -\frac{1}{2}$$

Example 1.6a Given the following function, find the roots and vertex.
$$f(x) = x^2 - 10x + 21$$

25

Solution Example 1.6a

Finding the roots

Method 1: factoring

$$(x - 3)(x - 7) = 0$$ -3 and -7 add into -10 and multiply into 21

$$x = 3 \text{ and } x = 7$$

Method 2: quadratic formula

$$x_1 = \frac{-(-10) + \sqrt{10^2 - 4(1)(21)}}{2(1)} = \frac{10 + 4}{2} = 7$$

$$x_2 = \frac{-(-10) - \sqrt{10^2 - 4(1)(21)}}{2(1)} = \frac{10 - 4}{2} = 3$$

Finding the vertex

$$= -\frac{-10}{2(1)} = 5$$

Example 1.6b   **Given the following function, find the roots and vertex.**

$$f(x) = (x - 4)^2 + 2$$

Solution Example 1.6b

Rewrite the function in the form of $f(x) = ax^2 + bx + c$

$$f(x) = x^2 - 8x + 16 + 2 = x_2 - 8x + 18$$

Use the quadratic formula

$$x = \frac{-(-8) + \sqrt{(-8)^2 - 4(1)(18)}}{2(1)} = \frac{8 + \sqrt{-8}}{2}$$

With the negative in the square root, this means that there are no real roots. That is, the function does not cross the x-axis.

But it still has a vertex

$$x = \frac{-b}{2a} = \frac{-(-8)}{2} = 4$$

Chapter 1.7 Graphing Quadratic Functions

In the same way that we graphed out linear functions, we can also graph out quadratic functions. Let's consider the following function

$$f(x) = -2x^2 + 4x - 10$$

To graph this out, we want to set up two columns, one with the values of x and the other with the resulting values of the function.

▲	A	B
1	x	f(x)
2		-10
3		-9
4		-8
5		-7
6		-6
7		-5
8		-4
9		-3
10		-2
11		-1
12		0
13		1
14		2

▲	A	B	C
1	x	f(x)	
2		-10	=-2*A2^2+4*A2-1(
3		-9	-208
4		-8	-170
5		-7	-136
6		-6	-106
7		-5	-80
8		-4	-58
9		-3	-40
10		-2	-26
11		-1	-16
12		0	-10
13		1	-8
14		2	-10

Then we can highlight the $f(x)$ and subsequent values and go to Insert > Chart > Line with Markers. Right click and Select Data. Then edit the horizontal axis to match and you should get a graph that looks similar to the following:

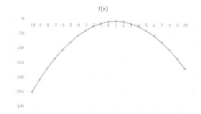

Notice that the function does not cross the x-axis. This would be an example of a quadratic function that does not have any real roots. Meaning that if you used the quadratic formula, you would get a negative value inside the square root. (Similar to Example 1.6b)

YouTube video graphing quadratic function: https://youtu.be/_4kjVsQB7vo

Chapter 1.8 Spreadsheet Model for Quadratic Functions

In this chapter we want to set up a spreadsheet that will combine Sections 1.6 and 1.7 within the same spreadsheet model. That is, we want to set up a spreadsheet that will allow us to calculate the roots and vertex along with graphing the function. The key to setting up this spreadsheet is to parameterize the equations within excel.

This spreadsheet will be one of the most useful spreadsheets you will use in this class. There will be many times where your work will be reduced if you can refer to this spreadsheet. I highly recommend that you become a master at setting up this spreadsheet model on your own.

Step 1: Set up spreadsheet with input cells and desired outputs.

	A	B	C	D	E
1	Quadratic Function:				
2	$f(x) = ax^2 + bx + c$				
3					
4		Parameters			
5	a			x-coordinate of vertex	
6	b			One root	
7	c			Second root	
8					
9	x	f(x)			
10					

This is set up to show the equation for a quadratic function and then to set up cells where you can insert values of the parameters of the quadratic function (again, the parameters in the quadratic function are the values for a, b, and c). The desired output will be the vertex and the two roots (where the function crosses the x-axis). Down below, will be the set up to graph the function. So I will have a column for the x values that you choose and the resulting value of the function.

Step 2: Fill in the spreadsheet with formulas for vertex and roots

Let's start with the vertex. The equation of the vertex is $x = -\dfrac{b}{2a}$. This is what we enter into the cell E5. Notice that we are reference the parameters from column B.

	A	B	C	D	E
1	Quadratic Function:				
2	$f(x) = ax^2 + bx + c$				
3					
4		Parameters			
5	a			x-coordinate of vertex	=-B6/(2*B5)
6	b			One root	
7	c			Second root	

When you type the formula in and hit enter, you should get the code #DIV/0!, this means that you are trying to divide by 0, which is bad. When the parameter cells are blank, Excel treats those as 0's, so you are dividing by 0 when the cells are blank.

If this bothers you, let's resolve it. Let's consider the following function:

$$f(x) = x^2 - 10x + 21.$$

Let's plug those numbers in for a, b, and c. With the vertex we know the answer should be 5. If you plug in 1, -10, and 21 in for the parameters, respectively, the answer you get in your Excel worksheet should be 5.

Now let's turn to the values of the roots. We found these values earlier in Example 1.6a, so we know the answer should be $x_1 = 3$ and $x_2 = 7$. In cells E6 and E7 we are going to put the two equations for the quadratic formula.

As a reminder, that formula is $x = \frac{-b \pm \sqrt{b^2 - 4ac}}{2a}$

The quadratic formula has two equations built into it, one where we add the square root and the other where we subtract the square root. It doesn't matter which one we call the first or second root, but the order of operation is going to be very very very very important. I will start first with the plus version of the quadratic formula. I enter it into Excel the following way:

	A	B	C	D	E	F	G
1	Quadratic Function:						
2	f(x) = ax² + bx + c						
3							
4		Parameters					
5	a	1		x-coordinate of vertex	5		
6	b	-10		On	=(-B6+SQRT(B6^2-4*B5*B7))/(2*B5)		
7	c	21		Second root			
8							

Notice the use of parenthesis, this is how you ensure that the order of operation is followed.

Now let's do the second equation of the quadratic formula

	A	B	C	D	E	F	G
1	Quadratic Function:						
2	f(x) = ax² + bx + c						
3							
4		Parameters					
5	a	1		x-coordinate of vertex	5		
6	b	-10		One root	7		
7	c	21		Sec	=(-B6-SQRT(B6^2-4*B5*B7))/(2*B5)		
8							

Some tips on setting up these formulas in your model
- SQRT( ) is the Excel formula for square foot
- The most common mistake I see is that the last parenthesis is not used.

- You cannot enter the plus square root equation of the quadratic formula into cell E6 and then copy and paste it into cell E7 and then change the plus to a minus. Excel uses references based on relative position, so if you want to copy-paste, you need to anchor each reference to a parameter.
- When setting this up, use quadratic function where you know the answer. This will allow you to check your work as you set it up. In this set up we used Example 1.6a to help us check our work.

Step 3: Set up values to graph function

Let's start by putting in potential values for x. I encourage you to start with -10 to 10 as your domain and then adjust it from there depending on the graph.

	x	f(x)
9		
10	-10	
11	-9	
12	-8	
13	-7	
14	-6	

Now we need to input the value of the function. But before we do, I want to remind you that Excel uses references based on relative position. So we want to reference the value of x that is one column to the left, but we want to use absolute referencing, or anchoring, to always reference the parameters.

	A	B	C
1	Quadratic Function:		
2	f(x) = ax² + bx + c		
3			
4		Parameters	
5	a	1	x-coordi
6	b	-10	One roo
7	c	21	Second
8			
9	x	f(x)	
10	-10	=$B$5*A10^2+$B$6*A10+$B$7	
11	-9		
12	-8		
13	-7		

To anchor, you can type the dollar signs, or when you click on the referenced cell, hit the F4 key and it will add the dollar signs for you.

Once you do this, you can copy and paste the formula all the way down.

Now to create the graph, highlight the cells for f(x) and go to the Data tab in the ribbon and insert line chart. (for this one, I will choose a line without markers)

Right click the graph and choose Select Data to change the horizontal axis values to match the values of the x column,

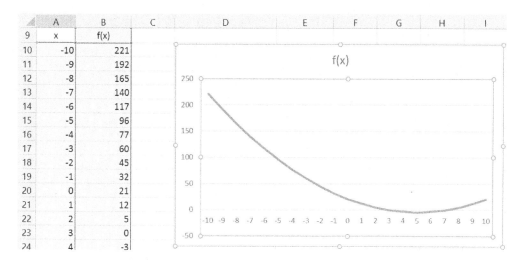

	A	B
9	x	f(x)
10	-10	221
11	-9	192
12	-8	165
13	-7	140
14	-6	117
15	-5	96
16	-4	77
17	-3	60
18	-2	45
19	-1	32
20	0	21
21	1	12
22	2	5
23	3	0
24	4	-3

Your graph should look like the one above.

We now have a spreadsheet model that will take a quadratic function and solve the values for the vertex, two roots, and graph the function.

We will reference this spreadsheet model as "Model for a Quadratic Function"

Example 1.8a. Given the function $f(x) = -2x^2 + 4x + 6$, **what is the vertex, the roots, and graph out the function. Copy and Paste your spreadsheet below.**

31

Solution Example 1.8a

All that needs to be done to solve this is to enter the new parameters:

$$a = -2, b = 4, \text{and } c = 6$$

Once you do this, everything is done for you.

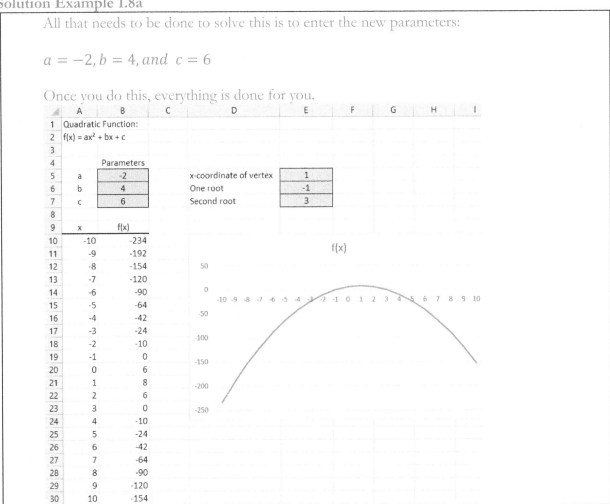

Example 1.8b Given the function $f(x) = 3x^2 - 6x - 10$, what is the vertex, the roots, and graph out the function

Solution Example 1.8b

Just enter the information into the spreadsheet you created for 1.8a and all the work is done for you.

However, if you look at the graph, most of the interesting parts of the graph happen between the x-values of -5 and 5. You can change the values of x to zoom into the key area of the graph.

To do so, type -5 in cell A10 and -4.5 into cell A11. Highlight these two cells and then double click on the lower right hand corner of the highlighted cells box. This will now change the values of x to go from -5 to 5 by 0.5 increments, which may give you a better depiction of where the function crosses the x-axis.

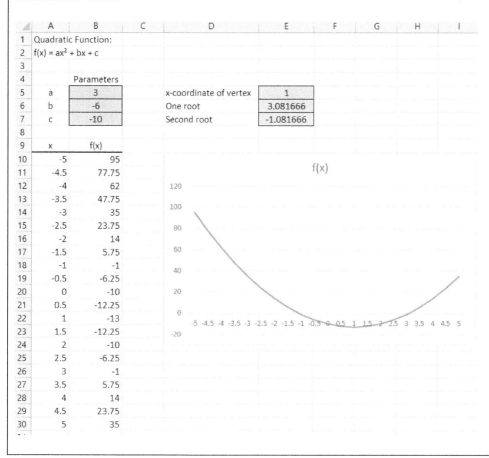

	A	B	C	D	E	F	G	H	I
1	Quadratic Function:								
2	$f(x) = ax^2 + bx + c$								
3									
4		Parameters							
5	a	3		x-coordinate of vertex	1				
6	b	-6		One root	3.081666				
7	c	-10		Second root	-1.081666				
8									
9	x	f(x)							
10	-5	95							
11	-4.5	77.75							
12	-4	62							
13	-3.5	47.75							
14	-3	35							
15	-2.5	23.75							
16	-2	14							
17	-1.5	5.75							
18	-1	-1							
19	-0.5	-6.25							
20	0	-10							
21	0.5	-12.25							
22	1	-13							
23	1.5	-12.25							
24	2	-10							
25	2.5	-6.25							
26	3	-1							
27	3.5	5.75							
28	4	14							
29	4.5	23.75							
30	5	35							

Example 1.8c. Given the function $f(x) = 3x^2 - 6x + 10$, what are the x-values when $f(x) = 0$?

Solution Example 1.8c.

Again, we just plug in the values of the parameters.

When you do so you get the following:

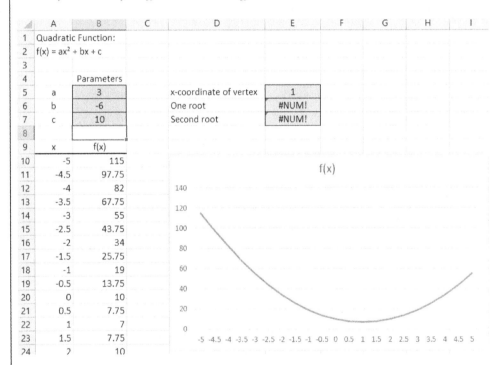

Notice that the roots get you #NUM!. This is not a trending twitter hashtag, this means that there are no roots.

When you look at the graph below you should be able to see this clearly, the function does not cross the x-axis.

Therefore, the answer for this example is that there are no values of x in which $f(x) = 0$

Chapter 1.9 Application: Profit Maximization

In this application, we want to take a classic economic example and set up a spreadsheet to solve it

Example 1.9a   Consider a firm (firm is fancy talk for a company) with the following information:

Inverse Demand Function	$P(Q) = 50 - 2Q$
Total Cost Function	$TC(Q) = 30 + 10Q$

Find the quantity that maximizes profits and graph out the Total Revenue, Total Costs, and the Profit Functions

There are two equations that will help you solve this problem:

(1) Profits = Total Revenue – Total Cost

(2) Total Revenue = Price x Quantity

We want to find the maximum profits, which uses the first equation, but we need the find Total Revenue first. So let's use the second equation to find Total Revenues

$TR = P \ x \ Q$ We are given P in the form of the inverse demand function
$TR = (50 - 2Q) \ x \ Q$
$TR = 50Q - 2Q^2$

We now have Total Revenue and the question gave us Total Cost, so we can now use the second equation. (Note: profit is represented by the Greek symbol pi π)

$\pi = TR - TC$
$\pi = [50Q - 2Q^2] - [30 + 10Q]$ Distribute negative through and collect like terms
$\pi = -2Q^2 + 40Q - 30$

To find where profits are maximized, you can use "SM Quadratic Function". The vertex is where profits are maximized, so the answer is Q*=10, this is where profits are maximized.

Next, we need to set up the spreadsheet to graph the different functions.
Let's start with the information we have: Q (from 0 to 20), the inverse demand function and the total cost function.

	A	B	C
1	Q	P	TC
2	0	50	30
3	1	48	40
4	2	46	50
5	3	44	60
6	4	42	70
7	5	40	80
8	6	38	90

For TR, create a column using the equation $TR = PQ$.

	A	B	C	D
1	Q	P	TC	TR
2	0	50	30	=B2*A2

For profits, we can use the formula of $\pi = TR - TC$.

36

	A	B	C	D	E
1	Q	P	TC	TR	Profits
2	0	50	30	0	=D2-C2
3	1	48	40		
4	2	46	50		

Copy-paste those two cells all the way down.

Now we can highlight the columns TC, TR, and profits. Go to Data > Insert > Line Chart. This will graph out all three functions and provide labels in the legend. Make sure to edit the horizontal axis. Add a Chart Title and you get something like this:

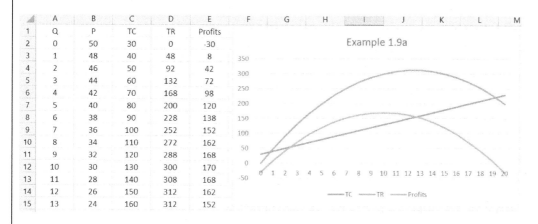

	A	B	C	D	E
1	Q	P	TC	TR	Profits
2	0	50	30	0	-30
3	1	48	40	48	8
4	2	46	50	92	42
5	3	44	60	132	72
6	4	42	70	168	98
7	5	40	80	200	120
8	6	38	90	228	138
9	7	36	100	252	152
10	8	34	110	272	162
11	9	32	120	288	168
12	10	30	130	300	170
13	11	28	140	308	168
14	12	26	150	312	162
15	13	24	160	312	152

YouTube video for Example 1.9a: https://youtu.be/Ywdncmw9P_Q

Example 1.9b Consider a firm with the following information:

$$P = 600 - 5Q$$
$$TC = 100Q + 10,500$$

Graph Total Revenue, Total Cost, and the Profit Functions

Solution Example 1.9b

You can set up the spreadsheet in a similar way that you did with Example 1.9a. If you set the range of Q's from 0 to 20 by 1's, you get a graph that looks like this:

	A	B	C	D	E
1	Q	P	TC	TR	Profits
2	0	600	10500	0	-10500
3	1	595	10600	595	-10005
4	2	590	10700	1180	-9520
5	3	585	10800	1755	-9045
6	4	580	10900	2320	-8580
7	5	575	11000	2875	-8125
8	6	570	11100	3420	-7680
9	7	565	11200	3955	-7245
10	8	560	11300	4480	-6820
11	9	555	11400	4995	-6405
12	10	550	11500	5500	-6000
13	11	545	11600	5995	-5605
14	12	540	11700	6480	-5220
15	13	535	11800	6955	-4845

The range of Q's is too small. We need to zoom out, or change the values of Q to see more of the graph. To do this, change the Q's to go from 0 to 100, counting by 5's. Doing so gives the following graph which better shows the functions.

	A	B	C	D	E
1	Q	P	TC	TR	Profits
2	0	600	10500	0	-10500
3	5	575	11000	2875	-8125
4	10	550	11500	5500	-6000
5	15	525	12000	7875	-4125
6	20	500	12500	10000	-2500
7	25	475	13000	11875	-1125
8	30	450	13500	13500	0
9	35	425	14000	14875	875
10	40	400	14500	16000	1500
11	45	375	15000	16875	1875
12	50	350	15500	17500	2000
13	55	325	16000	17875	1875
14	60	300	16500	18000	1500
15	65	275	17000	17875	875

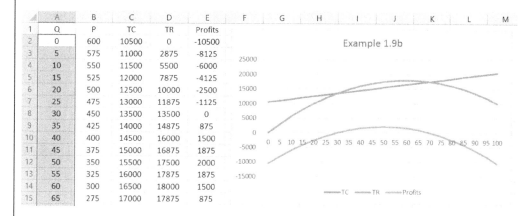

YouTube video for Example 1.9b: https://youtu.be/2lCQ49IwUwo

39

Chapter 1.10 Application: Costs

The goal for most companies is to maximize profits. To do this, there are two things they can do: 1) increase revenues and/or 2) decrease costs. Some companies have separate divisions or departments dedicated to each aspect. In this section, we are going to focus on costs.

Let's think about the different costs that a top-notch Mexican restaurant in Cedar City might face. Let's simplify things and consider that they produce only one dish: Chili Rellenos. One type of cost that the restaurant faces might include the lease of the building, buying the equipment in the kitchen, and the furniture in the dining area. All these costs are accrued even if they never produce a delicious chili relleno. We call these types of costs fixed costs. But if they do decide to make some chili rellenos, they will need to pay their chefs, they will need chilis and other ingredients for the chefs to cook, and they will need servers to take orders. All of these costs will vary based on how many orders are placed. These costs are called variable costs.

From these two types of costs, we can define other types of costs

Type of Cost	Definition
Fixed Costs	Costs that do not depend on how much is produced
Variable Costs	Costs that depends on the amount produced
Total Costs	Summation of fixed and variable costs
Marginal Costs	The incremental cost to produce on more unit
Average Costs	The cost per unit produced (cost divided by Q)

Let's add some numbers to our example of a Mexican restaurant. The restaurant has a fixed cost of $8,250 and it costs them $2.10 for each chili relleno to produce. From this information we could write out functions for each cost:

$$FC(Q) = 8,250 \qquad \text{Notice that it does not depend on Q}$$
$$VC(Q) = 2.10Q \qquad \text{Notice that this does depend on Q}$$

Combine these to get total costs
$$TC(Q) = 2.10Q + 8,250$$

For marginal cost, we have to ask how much is the incremental cost to produce one more chili relleno?
$$MC(Q) = 2.10$$

To find Average Total Cost, we would take our Total Cost and divide by Q:
$$ATC(Q) = \frac{2.10Q + 8,250}{Q}$$

Example 1.10a   Suppose that total cost is given by $TC(Q) = 50 + 25Q + 2Q^2$. Give the expressions for the following and evaluate each at $Q = 10$.

	Equation	Value when $Q = 10$
Fixed Costs		
Variable Costs		
Average Fixed Costs		
Average Variable Costs		
Average Total Costs		

Example 1.10b   Suppose a firm has to pay its supplier $P = 50 + .5Q$ per unit for its main input. In addition, the firm must pay transportation costs of $2.00 per unit and a tax of $3.00 per unit. What is the total cost function?

Solution Example 1.10a

$$TC(Q) = 50 + 25Q + 2Q^2$$

	Equation	Value when $Q = 10$
Fixed Costs	$FC(Q) = 50$	50
Variable Costs	$VC(Q) = 25Q + 2Q^2$	450
Average Fixed Costs	$AFC(Q) = \dfrac{50}{Q}$	5
Average Variable Costs	$AVC(Q) = \dfrac{25Q + 2Q^2}{Q}$	45
Average Total Costs	$ATC(Q) = \dfrac{50 + 25Q + 2Q^2}{Q}$	50

Solution Example 1.10b

Total production cost is the per-unit production cost times the number of units produced. To this, add the per-unit transportation cost time the number of units and the per-unit tax cost times the number of units

Mathematically:

$$TC(Q) = (50 + .5Q)Q + 2Q + 3Q = 55Q + .5Q^2$$

Chapter 1.11 Systems of Equations

Previously we were looking at functions that represented two variables and one equation. For example: $y = mx + b$. With systems of equations we want to look at multiple equations and solve for the variables.

If we look at the equation $y = 25 - 2x$ there are multiple solutions to this equation. For example, the points (10,15) satisfy this equation. As do the points (15,-5). In fact, there is a whole line of points that will satisfy the equation.

But what happens if we look at not one, but two equations

(i) $y = 25 - 2x$
(ii) $y = -2 + 3x$

The point (10,15) satisfies the first equation but not the second. If you plug 10 in for x in the second equation you get $-2 + 3(10) = 28$ which is not equal to 15.
When solving systems of equations, we are looking for an x and y that solves both equations.

There are several ways to do this. If we want to do it by hand, then we would set the two equations equal to each other and solve for x

$$25 - 2x = -2 + 3x$$
$$27 = 5x$$
$$x = 5.4$$
$$y = 14.2$$

we can then plug this x into either equation to get

So the solution to this system of equations is the point (5.4,14.2)

In order to solve a system of equations, it is necessary that there be at least as many equations as there are variables. In the example above, there were <u>two</u> equations and <u>two</u> variables. Therefore, we have a unique answer that solves this system.

But if we had just one equation and two variables, then the solution would not be unique but rather a whole set of solutions (those that are on the line).

As we add more variables and more equations, it becomes exponentially less fun to solve these by hand. That is why we can use a tool within Excel to solve systems of equations for us.
I introduce you to

Introduction to Solver

Solver should be on the far right when you click on the Data tab in the ribbon. If it is not there, here is how you can add it:

In the ribbon, click on File. On the left side of the screen at the bottom, click on "Options". This will open a new window, on the left of the window is "Add-ins", give that a click. Near the bottom click on "Go". Another window will open, click on the "Solver Add-in" box and then click "OK". Go to the Data tab and on the far right you should see the following:

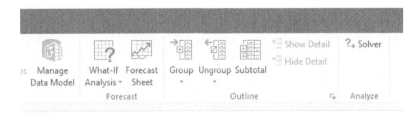

YouTube video on how to add Solver: https://youtu.be/f5k_iaAdQ6Q

Let's use Solver now to solve the previous example of a system of equations.

   (i) $y = 25 - 2x$
   (ii) $y = -2 + 3x$

In Excel, let's designate a cell for x. Below that cell, leave it blank and highlight it blue (that's my preference, but you can choose your own color). Then designate cells for each equation and insert the equations referencing the blue cell representing x.

	A	B
1	x	
2		
3	(i)	(ii)
4	25	=-2+3*A2

What we want to do is to choose an x that will make
   equation (i) = equation (ii)

We can rewrite this equation in the following way:
   equation (i) − equation (ii) = 0

If they equal each other, then the difference is 0.
We create a call for the difference of the two equations

	A	B	C
1	x		
2			
3	(i)	(ii)	Difference
4	25	-2	=A4-B4

Now we want to choose an x with the objective that the difference equals 0. This is the thought process that aligns with the set up used by Solver.

Go to Data > Solver and you should get the following window:

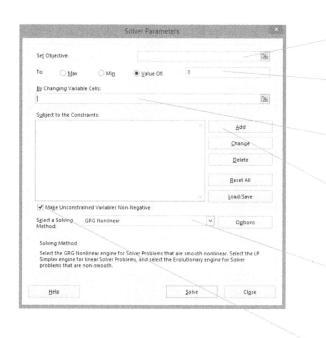

Here is where you reference the objective

You can designate three objectives: max, min, or set to a specific value

Reference your variable(s); that is what we want to choose to achieve the objective

We can add constraints, more on that later

We will talk about this later as well

The default is that your variable has to be positive, many times you may want to uncheck this box especially when the answer may be a negative number

For our example, it would look like this:

	A	B	C
1	x		
2			
3	(i)	(ii)	Difference
4	25	-2	27.00
5			
6			
7			

Solver Parameters

Set Objective: $C$4

To: ○ Max ○ Min ● Value Of: 0

By Changing Variable Cells:
$A$2

Click on "Solve" and then click "OK". Your answer should show that value of $x = 5.4$ solves the system with an answer of $y = 14.2$ for both equations

	A	B	C
1	x		
2	5.4		
3	(i)	(ii)	Difference
4	14.2	14.2	-1E-06

You may be concerned with the number that shows up in the difference cell. This number should be 0 but instead you are seeing this. This is not an error, it is just a very small number close to zero written in scientific notation. Written without scientific notation would show that the difference is -0.0000001. If you format the cell to a number, it will look like a 0 again.

YouTube video on intro to Solver: https://youtu.be/kftKQQ2B_6E

Below are a few examples for you to work through to practice setting up a spreadsheet and solve a system of equations using Solver.

Example 1.11a   **Use Solver to find the equilibrium price and quantity of the following supply and demand functions**

$$Q^S = 100 + \frac{1}{4}P \qquad\qquad Q^D = 400 - \frac{1}{2}P$$

Example 1.11b   **Use Solver to find the x value that solves this system of equations**

$$y = 120 - 6x \qquad\qquad y = 240 - 3x$$

Example 1.11c   **Use Solver to find the x value that solves this system of equations**

$$12x - 7y = 106 \qquad 8x + y = 82$$

Important Note: I highly recommend that you work each problem in a different worksheet in Excel. You can create new worksheets by click on the ⊕ button on the bottom of your worksheet. When you save your file, it will also save the last thing done in Solver for each worksheet. That way you can come back and see how you used Solver for each problem.

Solution Example 1.11a

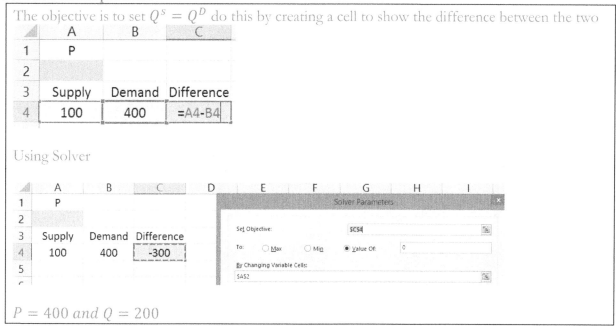

The objective is to set $Q^S = Q^D$ do this by creating a cell to show the difference between the two

	A	B	C
1	P		
2			
3	Supply	Demand	Difference
4	100	400	=A4-B4

Using Solver

$P = 400 \ and \ Q = 200$

Solution Example 1.11b

If you try to solve this, you should get an error saying that Solver could not find a feasible solution. This means that the two lines do not intersect or that there is not a solution to this system of equations.

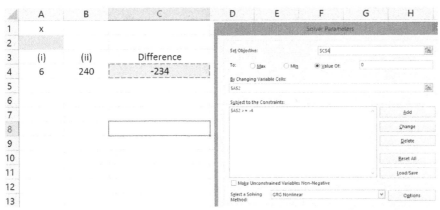

	A	B	C	D	E	F	G	H
1	x							
2	**10**							
3								
4	(i)	(ii)	Difference					
5	2	2	0					

$x = 10 \; and \; y = 2$

Let's look at another example.

$$(i) \; y = x^2 + 5x + 6 \qquad (ii) \; y = 240 - 3x$$

If we look at equation (i), we should be able to recognize that this is a quadratic function. This give the function a parabolic shape. Equation (ii) is a straight line, so it is possible that these functions intersect in two spots, not just one. Meaning that there may be two solutions to this system.

We can see that a by solving this by hand:

$$x^2 + 5x + 6 = 240 - 3x \qquad \text{Set the equations equal to each other}$$
$$x^2 + 8x - 234 = 0 \qquad \text{By collecting like terms}$$

We can use the quadratic function to solve this and if you use the SM Quadratic Function, you will see that there is a root on each side of the vertex. This will always be the case.
If we try to solve this system of equations in Solver, the algorithm used to solve the system within Solver may give us one of the two roots. Instead, we can use the vertex to create a constraint for Solver to give us both solutions.

We can set up a spreadsheet and use Solver in the same way as before. Except before we click "Solve" let's "Add" a constraint. The constraint we want to add is that our variable x is greater than the vertex.

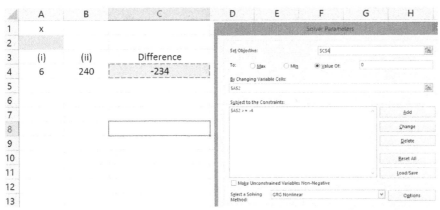

Note: if there is a possibility that your x is a negative number, make sure to uncheck this box.

Solution 1: $x = 11.81$ and $y = 204.57$

Now go back into Solver and "Change" the constraint. This time set the constraint to be $x \leq 4$

Solution 2: $x = -19.81$ and $y = 299.43$

As you can see, using constraints allows us to use Solver to work through more complex problems. While you may not think of the previous example as complex, so to convince you I present the following problem:

$$Q_1^S = 6P_1 - 8 \qquad\qquad Q_1^D = -5P_1 + P_2 + P_3 + 23$$
$$Q_2^S = 3P_2 - 11 \qquad\qquad Q_2^D = P_1 - 3P_2 + 2P_3 + 15$$
$$Q_3^S = 3P_3 - 5 \qquad\qquad Q_3^D = P_1 + 2P_2 - 4P_3 + 19$$

This is a system of equations in which three inter-related products. The subscript number represents which product we are referencing. For example Q_1^S refers to the quantity supplied of good 1. That is only dependent on the price of good 1. Q_1^D is the demand for good 1 and that depends on the price of good 1 and the price of the other two goods.

You can solve this by hand, it is not as fun as you think. It is examples like these that make Solver our one true love.

To solve this, we want to set
$$Q_1^S = Q_1^D$$
$$Q_2^S = Q_2^D$$
$$Q_3^S = Q_3^D$$

This is our objective and we achieve this by setting choose three variables, $P_1, P_2, and\ P_3$
We can set up the Spreadsheet with the following:

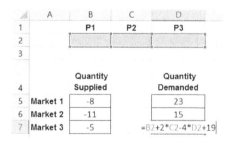

To create our objective we need to set $Q_1^S = Q_1^D$ which can be done by taking the difference between the supply and demand for each market

	A	B	C	D	E	F
1		P1	P2	P3		
2						
3						
4		Quantity Supplied		Quantity Demanded		Difference
5	Market 1	-8		23		31.0
6	Market 2	-11		15		26.0
7	Market 3	-5		19		=D7-B7

We now turn to Solver. But as we look to do this, Solver will let us do multiple variables, but only objective. So if we try to get the first market to clear (supply = demand) we would get the following:

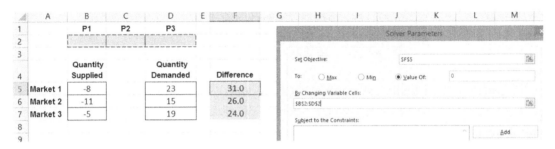

Note: to select multiple variables just hold down your mouse and highlight all three prices.

The solution will give us a set of prices such that Market 1 clears. But not the other two markets.

To get the other markets to clear, we need to incorporate them into our constraints.

	A	B	C	D	E	F	G	H	I	J	K	L	M
1		P1	P2	P3									
2		3	0	0						Solver Parameters			
3								Set Objective:		$F$5			
4		Quantity Supplied		Quantity Demanded		Difference		To: ○ Max ○ Min ● Value Of: 0					
5	Market 1	9		9		0.0		By Changing Variable Cells:					
6	Market 2	-11		18		28.8		$B$2:$D$2					
7	Market 3	-5		22		26.8		Subject to the Constraints:					
8								$F$6 = 0			Add		
9								$F$7 = 0					
10											Change		

By adding these constraints, we can get all three markets to clear

	P1	P2	P3	
	4	7	6	
	Quantity Supplied		Quantity Demanded	Difference
Market 1	16		16	0.0
Market 2	10		10	0.0
Market 3	13		13	0.0

So when we have multiple objectives we need to incorporate constraints to account for each one.

YouTube video for a 3x3 system of equations: https://youtu.be/g5S9JCArBYE

Chapter 2
Calculus

What is Calculus?

Cape Kiwanda is located on the Oregon Coast just
north of Pacific City. In addition to a beautiful view
of the ocean, a marine garden, great winds to fly a
kite, and ability to park your car on the beach, Cape
Kiwanda is best known for is ginormous sand hill
(pictured to the right). It takes 15 minutes and quads
of an Olympian just to arduously make your way to
the summit. But it takes a mere 20 seconds to race all
the way down, that is if you don't lose your balance
and fall. Then it takes about 40 seconds to roll to the
bottom.

Photo by Terry Richard of The Oregonian

What does Cape Kiwanda have to do with calculus? Absolutely everything.

Calculus is the mathematical study of change. In the case of Cape Kiwanda, we can study the change
in height for each step we take. As you take that first step, the height you have risen increases. And
with each additional step you take the height continues to rise.

How do you know when you get to the top? It is when you take a step and and you don't get any
higher.

Why is running down so much more fun than climbing up? It is because each step you take the
heigh decreases. Gravity begins to work with you as you begin to flail your arms realizing that you
are about to lose your balance.

We can relate this back to what we learned in algebra. In the algebra section we introduced the
equation of $y = mx + b$. We called m the slope which measures the change in y for a change in x.
Even though this equation is for a straight line and the sand hill is more curved shaped, we can
apply that same principle.

When you first start climbing up the hill, the slope of the hill is positive. When you reach the top,
there is no change in height for your next step, so the slope is zero. Then as you run down, the slope
of the hill is negative.

That is calculus. In this section of calculus, we are going to analyze different settings with the goal to
look at how y changes with a change in x. We will call this differential calculus.

Rather than look at a large sand hill, let's look at an example that analyzes sales and advertising. First, let's look at different ways in which we can graphically show the relationship between sales and advertising.

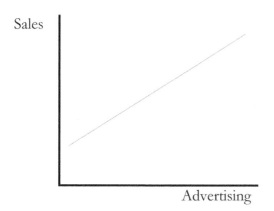

In this scenario, we can look at the slope to tell us the relationship between sales and advertising. The interpretation of the slope is the change in sales for a change in advertising (change in y for a change in x). In this case, it is positive; meaning that if you increase advertising sales will increase.

Rather than a straight line, the classic S-shape curve might be a better representation of the relationship between sales and advertising (as shown below).

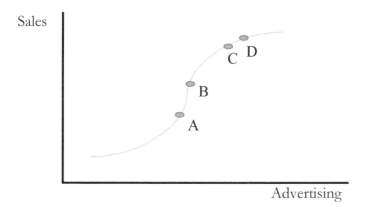

In this scenario, if we look at the slope between points A and B, we would use the same interpretation. The slope is the change in sales for a change in advertising (change in y for a change in x). The slope between C and D has the exact same interpretation, change in sales for a change in advertising.

But you will notice that the slope between those two points are not the same. The slope between A and B is much steeper than between C and D. That is increasing advertising from A to B increase sales more than changing advertising from C to D.

Technically, a line that connects two points on a function is called a **Secant**. You can use the equation for slope, $\frac{y_2-y_1}{x_2-x_1}$, to find the slope of the secant line.

Slope of Secant Line $= \frac{y_2-y_1}{x_2-x_1}$

or written slightly different

Slope of Secant Line $= \frac{f(x_2)-f(x_1)}{x_2-x_1}$

Example 2.1a   **Given the function $f(x) = x^2$, find the slope of the secant line between $x = 2$ and $x = 4$.**

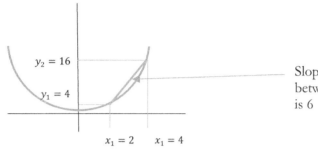
Example 2.1a   **Given the function $f(x) = x^2 + 6x - 5$, find the slope of the secant line between $x = 2$ and $x = 4$.**

What if we want to find the slope of the function at a single point? We can't use the old equation of slope because we don't have two points. We want to find the change in sales for a change in advertising at point A (see below). A line that touches the function at a single point is called a **Tangent**. We want to estimate the slope of a tangent line.

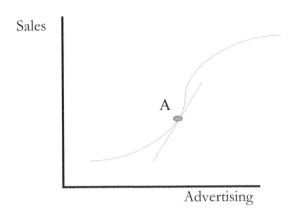

To find the slope of the tangent, let's start with two points and find the slope of the secant line. Consider the function below, we want to find the slope of the function when $x = 2$.

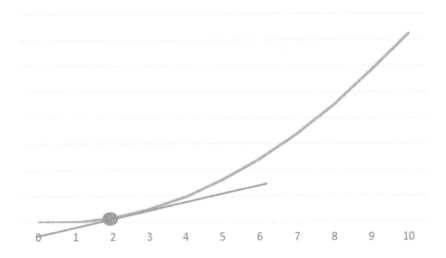

So let's choose a second point, $x_2 = 10$ and find the slope of the secant line between these two points.

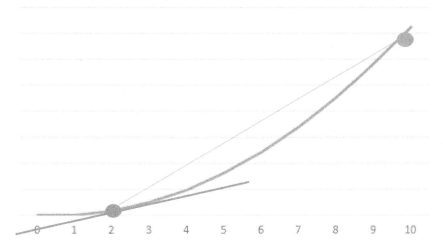

The slope of the secant line can be used as an approximation of the slope of the function when $x = 2$. It may not be a good approximation. So instead of choosing $x_2 = 10$ choose and x_2 that is closer to 2. In the figure below let's choose $x_2 = 5$

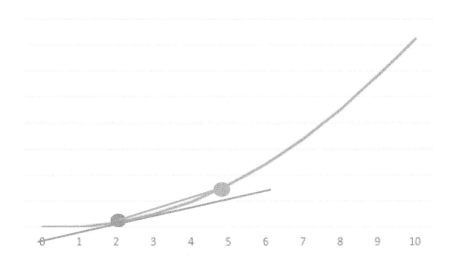

Now the slope of the Secant line is a slightly better approximation of the slope of the tangent line. As we choose an x_2 that gets closer and closer to the point of the function where we want to estimate the slope, the slope of the secant line will get progressively closer to the slope of the tangent line.

Example 2.2a   Using the function $f(x) = x^2$ set up an Excel Spreadsheet that shows how choosing an x_2 that gets closer and closer to $x = 2$ shows that the slope of the secant line converges to 4.

Solution Example 2.2a

Create a column for x, which is a column full of the number 2

Create a second column for x_2, each time letting x_2 get closer and closer to 2

(*Note: but x_2 can never equal 2)

A third column will use the formula for the slope of the secant line

$$\frac{y_2 - y_1}{x_2 - x_1}$$

The final spreadsheet should look like this:

x	x2	slope of secant
2	10	12
2	5	7
2	3	5
2	2.5	4.5
2	2.25	4.25
2	2.1	4.1
2	2.01	4.01
2	2.001	4.001
2	2.0001	4.0001

Notice that as x_2 gets closer to x, the slope of the secant line converges to 4

Now let's formalize this process with some mathematical equations. We will start with the slope of the secant and then let x_2 get really closer to x.

$$Slope\ of\ Secant\ Line = \frac{f(x_2) - f(x)}{x_2 - x}$$

Here we can define $\Delta x = x_2 - x$ and we can rewrite that as $x_2 = \Delta x + x$

We will substitute these into the slope of the secant line so we can get rid of x_2

$$Slope\ of\ Secant\ Line = \frac{f(x + \Delta x) - f(x)}{\Delta x}$$

As x_2 gets closer to x, Δx is getting closer to 0. Now it cannot actually equal 0, since that would make the denominator 0, and you cannot divide by 0. So we want Δx to get really, really close to 0 without actually getting to 0. That is the definition of the slope of the tangent line

$$Slope\ of\ Tangent\ line = \lim_{\Delta x \to 0} \frac{f(x + \Delta x) - f(x)}{\Delta x}$$

The term, $\lim_{\Delta x \to 0}$ means that we are taking the limit as Δx gets close to 0 without ever actually being equal to 0.

With this equation, we can find the slope of a function at a given point.

Example 2.2b Given the function $f(x) = 3x^2$ find the slope of the tangent line when $x = 2$

Solution Example 2.2b

Apply the equation of the slope of the tangent line

$$Slope\ T = \lim_{\Delta x \to 0} \frac{f(x+\Delta x)-f(x)}{\Delta x}$$

$f(x + \Delta x)$ means that where you see x in the function you insert $x + \Delta x$

$$Slope\ T = \lim_{\Delta x \to 0} \frac{3(x+\Delta x)^2-3x^2}{\Delta x} \qquad \text{foil out the squared term}$$

$$Slope\ T = \lim_{\Delta x \to 0} \frac{3(x^2+2x\Delta x+\Delta x^2)-3x^2}{\Delta x} \qquad \text{distribute the 3 through the equation}$$

$$Slope\ T = \lim_{\Delta x \to 0} \frac{(3x^2+6x\Delta x+3\Delta x^2)-3x^2}{\Delta x} \qquad \text{then collect like terms}$$

$$Slope\ T = \lim_{\Delta x \to 0} \frac{(3x^2-3x^2+\Delta x(6x+3\Delta x))}{\Delta x} \qquad \text{the } 3x^2 \text{ will cancel each other out}$$

$$Slope\ T = \lim_{\Delta x \to 0} \frac{(\Delta x(6x+3\Delta x))}{\Delta x} \qquad \text{now we can cancel a } \Delta x \text{ on the top and bottom}$$

$Slope\ T = \lim_{\Delta x \to 0} 6x + 3\Delta x$ with the Δx eliminated in the denominator, we can now let Δx be zero

$Slope\ T = 6x \qquad$ we evaluate it at $x = 2$

$Slope\ T = 12$

See Videos: https://www.youtube.com/watch?v=HFpGP94cYXU
https://www.youtube.com/watch?v=I19-L200ZOM

Example 2.2c **Set up an Excel spreadsheet to show that for the function**
$f(x) = 3x^2$ the slope converges to 6x when Δx gets closer to 0.

x	x2	slope of secant
2	10	36
2	5	21
2	3	15
2	2.5	13.5
2	2.25	12.75
2	2.1	12.3
2	2.01	12.03
2	2.001	12.003
2	2.0001	12.0003

Example 2.2d   Given the function $f(x) = -2x^2 - 4$, what is the slope of the tangent line when $x = -2$

)

Solution Example 2.2d

$f(x) = -2x^2 - 4$

$Slope\ T = \lim\limits_{\Delta x \to 0} \dfrac{f(x+\Delta x)-f(x)}{\Delta x}$

$Slope\ T = \dfrac{\lim\limits_{\Delta x \to 0}\left((-2(x+\Delta x)^2-4)-(-2x^2-4)\right)}{\Delta x}$

$= \dfrac{\lim\limits_{\Delta x \to 0}\left((-2(x^2+2x\Delta x+\Delta x^2)-4)-(-2x^2-4)\right)}{\Delta x}$

$= \dfrac{\lim\limits_{\Delta x \to 0}\left((-2x^2-4x\Delta x-2\Delta x^2)-4)+2x^2+4\right)}{\Delta x}$

$= \dfrac{\lim\limits_{\Delta x \to 0}\left((-4x\Delta x-2\Delta x^2))\right)}{\Delta x}$

$= \lim\limits_{\Delta x \to 0} -4x - 2\Delta x$

$= -4x$ when $x = -2$

$= 8$

Chapter 2.3 Application: Secant and Tangent Line

Consider the following graph that shows your drive from Cedar City to St. George.

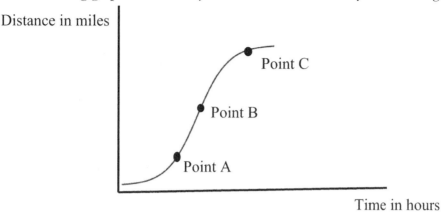

When would a police officer pull you over and what is the first question that you will be asked? This scenario helps illustrate the difference between the secant line and tangent.

The slope of the secant line gives the *average* rate of change.

The slope of the tangent line give the *instantaneous* rate of change.

So let's start with the set of questions in reverse order. When pulled over the first question, based on my experience has been, do you know how fast you were going?

The question is not what was your average speed since you left Cedar City? That is asking for the slope of the secant line (average rate of change). No, the officer wants to know how fast you were going the moment that the radar gun clocked you. The officer is asking about your speed at a given moment (the instantaneous rate of change of miles per hour)

With that, we can now answer the first question, when are you most likely to get pulled over? It is when the slope at a given point is the highest. This happens at Point B, also known as the Black Ridge.

Chapter 2.4 The Derivative

The derivative of a function $f(x)$ is defined as

$$\text{Derivative of } f(x) = \lim_{\Delta x \to 0} \frac{f(x+\Delta x)-f(x)}{\Delta x}$$

This should look really familiar, this is the slope of the tangent line. This means that the derivative of a function is the slope of the function at a given point.

There are several notations for the derivative of function $f(x)$

$$f'(x) \qquad \frac{df(x)}{dx}$$

So to go back to Example 2.2b, instead of asking what is the slope of the tangent line, we could instead ask,

(1) given the function $f(x) = 3x^2$ what is $f'(x)$?

Or

(2) Given the function $f(x) = 3x^2$ what is $\frac{df(x)}{dx}$?

> Note: The notation for a derivative for these two examples are identical

Then answer to both questions is $6x$.

Rather than have to apply the equation with limits and go through the long process. There are some shortcut rules you can follow that lead to the exact same answer, only faster. #yourewelcome

Rules of Differentiation

Rule (1) The Constant Function Rule – the slope of a constant function is 0

$$f(x) = k$$
$$f'(x) = 0 \text{ or } \frac{df(x)}{dx} = 0$$

Examples

$f(x) = 5$ $f(x) = -6$
$f'(x) = 0 \text{ or } \frac{df(x)}{dx} = 0$ $f'(x) = 0$

Rule (2) The Linear Function Rule – the derivative of a linear function is the slope (m)

$f(x) = mx + b$
$f'(x) = m$

Examples

$f(x) = 4x + 2$ $f(x) = -2x + 11$
$f'(x) = 4$ $f'(x) = -2$

Rule (3) The Power Function Rule

$f(x) = kx^n$
$f'(x) = n * kx^{n-1}$

Examples

$f(x) = 4x^2$ $f(x) = -2x^3$
$f'(x) = 8x$ $f'(x) = -6x^2$

Rule (4) The Rule for Sums and Differences

$f(x) = g(x) \pm h(x)$
$f'(x) = g'(x) \pm h'(x)$

Examples

$f(x) = 4x - 8x^2$ $f(x) = 3x^2 + 4x^3$
$f'(x) = 4 - 16x$ $f'(x) = 6x + 12x^2$

Rule (5) The Product Rule

$f(x) = g(x)h(x)$
$f'(x) = g'(x)h(x) + g(x)h'(x)$

Examples

$f(x) = 4x^2(3x - 1)$ $f(x) = (x + 2)(x^2 - 1)$
$f'(x) = 8x(3x - 1) + 4x^2(3)$ $f'(x) = 1(x^2 - 1) + (x + 2)(2x)$

Rule (6)   The Quotient Rule

$f(x) = \frac{g(x)}{h(x)}$

$f'(x) = \frac{h(x)g'(x) - g(x)h'(x)}{h(x)^2}$

Examples

$$f(x) = \frac{x^2 - 1}{3x}$$

$$f'(x) = \frac{2x(3x) - (x^2 - 1)3}{[3x]^2}$$

Note: to help you remember this rule, think lo-d-hi, hi-d-lo, over lolo

That is low (denominator) di-hi (derivative of numerator) minus hi (numerator) di-lo (dertivative of the denominator) divided by lolo (denominator times denominator)

See the videos for rules of differentiation: https://www.youtube.com/watch?v=6Kx5Vgt5x5c
https://www.youtube.com/watch?v=ta7SSV8Yz-k

Rule (7) The Chain Rule

$$f(x) = g\big(h(x)\big)$$
$$f'(x) = g'\big(h(x)\big)h'(x)$$

> Note: It is not required that you learn the chain rule for this course. This rule is widely used in many business applications. Trust me, this is one of the coolest derivatives you will ever learn, I mean Snoop Dog type cool

Chapter 2.5 Higher Order Derivatives and the Shape of Functions

The first derivative provides the instantaneous rate of change. But we can take higher order derivatives (the derivative of the derivative, also called the second derivative) which provides information on how the rate of change is changing.

Confused with that last statement? Consider this, let the function be distance as a function of time, call it d(t). The first derivative is the change in distance for a change in time at a given time, or what we call speed. The second derivative tells the change in speed (the first derivative) at a given time, or what we call acceleration. If the second derivative is positive, then speed is increasing (accelerating) or if the second derivative is negative then speed is decreasing (decelerating).

As such, two cars may have the same speed at a given point (same first derivative) but they may have different second derivatives because one is speeding up (second derivative is positive) and another may be slowing down (second derivative is negative). Or it may be that both second derivatives are positive, but one cars is accelerating faster than the other, even if they are going the same speed at the given point.

The second derivative is typically denoted $f''(x)$ or $\frac{d^2 f(x)}{dx^2}$

Higher order derivatives can also be taken and they follow a similar notation.

Example 2.5a Given the function $f(x) = 3x^4$, find the first and second derivatives.

Examples 2.5b   **Given the function of $f(x) = -4x^2 + 6x - 12$, find the first and second derivatives.**

Solution Example 2.5a

$$f(x) = 3x^4$$
$$f'(x) = 12x^3$$
$$f''(x) = 36x^2$$

Solution Example 2.5b

$$f(x) = -4x^2 + 6x - 12$$
$$f'(x) = -8x + 6$$
$$f''(x) = -8$$

Again, the first derivative indicates whether a function is increasing or decreasing; the second derivative indicates how fast the function is increasing or decreasing. Additionally, the second derivative can show if the function is concave or convex.

Concave: $f''(x) < 0$

A concave function looks like an upside down U. Two ways to remember this, concave functions look like ∩. Which kind of looks like a cave. The other way, is that if the second derivative is negative, then the function looks like a frowny face.

Convex: $f''(x) > 0$

A convex function is an upright U. You can remember this because the second derivative is positive and that makes you happy, so the function looks like a smiley face.

See Videos: https://www.youtube.com/watch?v=XMmbd7zc-fg
https://www.youtube.com/watch?v=eVyL-0jHV0s

Example 2.5c   **Determine whether the following function is (1) increasing, decreasing, or stationary at $x = 3$ and (2) concave or convex at $x = 3$:**

$$f(x) = x^3 - 4x^2 - 9x + 19$$

(1) $\dfrac{dy}{dx} = 3x^2 - 8x - 9$

Evaluate the function at x = 3

$= 3(3)^2 - 8(3) - 9 = 27 - 24 - 9 = -6$

So we would say that the function is decreasing at $x = 3$

(2) $\dfrac{d^2y}{dx^2} = 6x - 8$

Evaluate this when x = 3

$= 6(3) - 8 = 10$ which is greater than 0. Thus the function is convex

What if the second derivative is not positive or negative? Great question, if the second derivative is equal to 0 or undefined for point a, then we call that point an **inflection point**. An inflection point is where the function changes from concave to convex or vice a versa.

Consider the following function $f(x) = x^3$
Graphed out from $x = -5$ to $x = 5$ looks like what you see to your right.

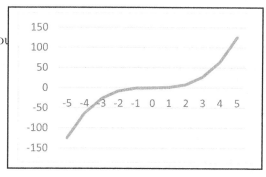

From -5 to 0 the function is concave (frowny face) and from 0 to 5 it is convex (happy face).

The first derivative is $f'(x) = 3x^2$
The second derivative is $f''(x) = 6x$
At $x = 0, f''(x) = 6(0) = 0.$

This is the inflection point. Or the point where the function goes from concave to convex.

Example 2.6a   Based on data from 1993 to 2002, the annual sales of Starbucks Corporation may be modeled by

$$s(t) = 29.23t^2 + 79.33t + 177.4$$

Where $s(t)$ are sales in millions of dollars and t is the number of years since the end of 1993.

(a)   Interpret the meaning of $s(9)$

(b)   Interpret the meaning of $s'(9)$

(c)   Use $s(9)$ and $s'(9)$ to *estimate* sales in year 2003.

Solution Example 2.6a

(a)   Interpret the meaning of $s(9)$

The model predicts that in 2002 annual sales were about $3,259 million

(b)   Interpret the meaning of $s'(9)$

The model units of the derivative are millions per year. So, $s'(9) = 605.47$. This means that in 2002, sales were increasing at the rate of $605.47 million dollars in that year.

(c)   Use $s(9)$ and $s'(9)$ to *estimate* sales in year 2003.

Assuming sales continue to increase at the rate of $605.47/year, they will be approximately 3,259 + 605.47 = 3,864.47 in 2003.

Chapter 2.7 Optimizing Functions Using Derivatives

We can use derivatives to maximize or minimize a function. We call these points relative extrema; it is a little influence that the X-games have had on mathematics.

A relative extrema is the x value that makes the first derivative equals 0 or mathematically $f(x) = 0$. Again the first derivative tells us the slope at a given point, so when the first derivative is equal to 0, that means the function has no slope. This occurs when you are at the very maximum of the function or the very minimum.

Two possible relative extrema

Figure A.   Figure B.

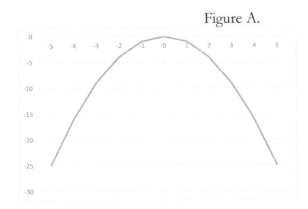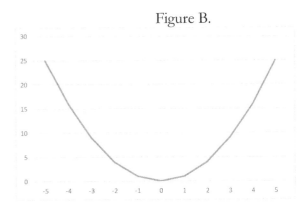

In Figure A, the relative extrema occurs when $x = 0$. The slope of the tangent line is 0, or the derivative is equal to 0 when $x = 0$. The same is true for Figure B.

Figure A is the function $f(x) = -x^2$ Figure B is the function $f(x) = x^2$

$f'(x) = -2x$ $f'(x) = -2x$

Set that equal to zero and solve for x   Set that equal to zero and solve for x
$-2x = 0$ $2x = 0$
$x^* = 0$ $x^* = 0$

The first derivative will provide the value of x that optimizes the function, or the relative extrema, but it is the second derivative that will tell you if the x value is a maximum or minimum. So here is the rule to find relative extrema and to determine if it is a maximum or minimum.

See Videos: https://www.youtube.com/watch?v=0kRPkLlwiCc

	Maximum	Minimum
First order condition	$f'(x) = 0$	$f'(x) = 0$
Second order condition	$f''(x) < 0$	$f''(x) > 0$

Example 2.7a   Optimize this function and show if the relative extrema is a max or a min
$$f(x) = -2x^2 + 24x - 96$$

Example 2.7b for the following function, find the relative extrema and determine whether each corresponds to a relative minimum or a relative maximum
$$f(x) = 2x^3 - 18x^2 + 48x - 29$$

$f(x) = -2x^2 + 24x - 96$
$f'(x) = -4x + 24$ set the first derivative equal to 0 and solve for x
$-4x + 24 = 0$
$x^* = 6$ the * means that this x optimizes the function

Check out the second derivative to show if it is max or min
$f''(x) = -4 < 0$ So this is a relative max.

Solution Example 2.7b

$f'(x) = 6x^2 - 36x + 48 = 6(x - 2)(x - 4)$ set it equal to zero
$f'(x) = 0$ → $x^* = 2, x^* = 4$

Take second derivative
$f''(x) = 12x - 36$

Plug in the values of x^*
$f''(2) = -12$ $x = 2$ corresponds to a relative max
$f''(4) = 12$ $x = 4$ corresponds to a relative min

See Videos: https://www.youtube.com/watch?v=0kRPkLlwiCc

Example 2.7c   **Optimize the following function with calculus**
$$f(x) = -5x^4 + 20x^3 + 280^2 - 19$$

Solution Example 2.7c

$$f'(x) = -20x^3 + 60x^2 + 560x = 0$$
$$f'(x) = -20x(x^2 - 3x - 28) = 0$$
$$f'(x) = -20x(x + 4)(x - 7) = 0$$

critical values: $x^* = 0$ $x^* = -4$ $x^* = 7$

Take second derivative
$$f''(x) = -60x^2 + 120x + 560$$

Plug in the critical values to see which are min and max's

$f''(x = -4) = -880 < 0$ relative max

$f''(x = 0) = 560 > 0$ relative min

$f''(x = 7) = -1540 < 0$ relative max

In summary, to optimize a function follow these 4 steps

(1) Take the first derivative
(2) Set it equal to zero
(3) Solve for the optimal value of x.
(4) Check the second order condition to show if it is a relative minimum or relative maximum.

We can use derivatives to help us in making business decisions. For example, if I know the demand function for the good I am producing, I can determine the quantity to produce to maximize revenues.

Consider the following inverse demand function $P = 100 - 2Q$
I can use the demand function to create a function for total revenue by using the following formula

$$\text{Total Revenue} = \text{Price} \times \text{Quantity}$$
$$\text{or}$$
$$\text{TR} = \text{PQ}$$

The inverse demand function is what we can use for Price (P). In this case:
$TR = PQ = (100 - 2Q)Q$
$TR = 100Q - 2Q^2$

To maximize a function, we go back to the steps
   (1) Take the first derivative $TR' = 100 - 4Q$
   (2) Set it equal to zero $100 - 4Q = 0$
   (3) Solve for x, in this case we will solve for Q $Q^* = 25$

So the quantity you would produce to maximize revenues would be 25.

Now we can apply the last step just to show that this is a relative max
   (4) Check second order conditions $TR'' = -4 < 0$
As such it is indeed a relative max.

In the same way that we can maximize revenue, we can also minimize costs. Consider a cost function that has two parts
     FC: $fixed\ costs = 250$
     VC: $variable\ costs = \frac{1}{2}Q^2 - 46Q$

We can find the quantity that will minimize total costs.
     $Total\ Costs = FC + VC = \frac{1}{2}Q^2 - 46Q + 250$
We can follow the same steps of function optimization
     $TC' = Q - 46 = 0$
     $Q^* = 46$
     Check second order conditions
     $TC'' = 1 > 0$ so it is a relative min

Most companies don't want to just maximize revenues or minimize costs in isolation, what they really want to do is to maximize profits. We can use the following formula to combine total revenue and total cost to create profits:

$$\text{Profits} = \text{Total Revenue} - \text{Total Cost}$$
$$\text{or}$$
$$\pi = TR - PQ$$

Intuition behind the concept

This is a representation of the profit function; it is an upside down parabola.

The highest point, or the maximum, is where the tangent line is equal to 0.

Thus, we take the first derivative and set it equal to zero to find the quantity that maximizes profits.

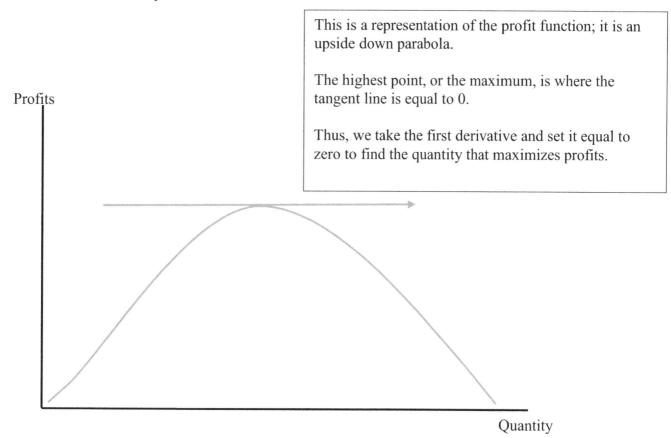

Profits

Quantity

Example 2.8a Calculate the quantity that maximizes profits with the information provided below:

Inverse Demand Function:	$P = 80 - 2Q$
Fixed Costs:	50
Variable Costs:	$3Q^2 + 10Q$

Solution Example 2.8a

$$\pi(Q) = TR(Q) - TC(Q) =$$
$$\pi(Q) = [80Q - 2Q^2] - [3Q^2 + 10Q + 50]$$
$$\pi(Q) = -5Q^2 + 70Q - 50$$

To find the profit-maximizing level of output:

$$\frac{d\pi}{dQ} = -10Q + 70 = 0$$

$$Q^* = 7$$

Some important economic terms are defined by using derivatives. Let's look at each of these:

Marginal Revenue (MR)

The definition of marginal revenue is the change in total revenue for producing one more unit. This is similar to the definition of derivative.

Instead of writing the derivative like this TR', you can write it out using a different notation but it means the exact same thing:

$\frac{dTR}{dQ}$ this says, find the derivative of TR when Q is your variable. Or better interpreted, it is the change in total revenue for a change in quantity. Remember, that a derivative is the slope of a function at a given point, so this notation is similar to $\frac{\Delta y}{\Delta x}$

Bringing it together, this is how we define MR using derivatives:

$$MR = \frac{dTR}{dQ}$$

Marginal Cost (MC)

The definition of marginal cost is the change in total cost for a change in quantity. Using the same rationale as discussed above, we get this definition:

$$MC = \frac{dTC}{dQ}$$

Profit Maximization

In principles of microeconomics, you learned that in any type of market the way to maximize profits is to set MR = MC. We can use derivatives to prove that this is indeed always the case. First, let's start with a definition of profits

$$\pi = TR - TC$$

To maximize profits, you would take the first derivative and set it equal to 0.

$$\pi' = TR' - TC' = 0 \qquad \text{(this is using Derivative Rule 4)}$$

Now we can use the definitions marginal revenue and marginal cost to make the following substitution

$$\pi' = MR - MC = 0$$
$$MR = MC$$

This means that you set marginal revenue equal to marginal cost, solve for quantity and this is the quantity that will maximize profits.

Here are a few examples to apply these principles.

Example 2.8b   Given that $P = 80 - 2Q$. Derive

    (a) $TR(Q)$

    (b) $MR(Q)$

    (c) $MR(4)$

    (d) $MR(5)$

    (e)   Show how $\frac{\Delta TR}{\Delta Q}$ is related

Solution Example 2.8b

(a) $$TR(Q) = PQ = (80 - 2Q)Q = 80Q - 2Q^2$$
(b) $$MR(Q) = \frac{dTR}{dQ} = 80 - 4Q$$
(c) $$MR(4) = 80 - 4(4) = 64$$
(d) $$MR(5) = 80 - 4(5) = 60$$

(e) From $Q = 4$ to $Q = 5$ we have

$$\frac{\Delta TR}{\Delta Q} = \frac{[80(5) - 2(5)^2] - [80(4) - 2(4)^2]}{5 - 4} = \frac{350 - 288}{1} = 62$$

This is the *average* change in revenue from Q=4 to Q=5; note that it is midway between the instantaneous rate of change at Q=4 and the instantaneous rate of change at Q=5, as given by the respective derivatives.

Example 2.8c   Given a total cost function: $TC(Q) = 3Q^2 + 10Q + 50$
(a)   Derive MC(Q)
(b) MC(2)
(c) MC(3)
(d)   show how $\frac{\Delta TC}{\Delta Q}$ is related to MC(2) and MC(3)

Solution Example 2.8c

(a) $$MC(Q) = \frac{dTC}{dQ} = 6Q + 10$$

(b) $$MC(2) = 6(2) + 10 = 22$$

(c) $$MC(3) = 6(3) + 10 = 28$$

From $Q = 2$ to $Q = 3$, we have

$$\frac{\Delta TC}{\Delta Q} = \frac{[TC(3) - TC(2)]}{[3-2]} = \frac{[3(3^2) + 10(3) + 50] - [3(2^2) + 10(2) + 50]}{1}$$

$$= \frac{107 - 82}{1} = 25$$

This is the *average* change in cost from $Q = 2$ to $Q = 3$; note that it is about the midway between the instantaneous rate of change at $Q = 2$ and the instantaneous rate of change at $Q = 3$, as given by the respective derivatives.

Example 2.8d   **Given the demand function $P = 80 - 2Q$ and the total cost function $TC(Q) = 3Q^2 + 10Q + 50$, what is the quantity that maximizes profits. Show that that quantity is indeed a maximum and not a minimum**

Solution Example 2.8d

$$\pi = TR - TC = (80 - 2Q)Q - [3Q^2 + 10Q + 50]$$

$$= 80Q - 2Q^2 - 3Q^2 - 10Q - 50 = -5Q^2 + 70Q - 50$$

$$\pi' = -10Q + 70 = 0$$

$$Q^* = 7$$

Check second order conditions

$$\pi'' = -10 < 0 \qquad \text{therefore it is a relative max}$$

Example 2.8e Given the following functions, use the equation MR=MC to find the point where profits are maximized.

$$P(Q) = 800 - 7Q$$

$$TC(Q) = 2Q^3 - Q^2 + 80Q + 150$$

Solution Example 2.8e

$$TR(Q) = (800 - 7Q)Q = 800Q - 7Q^2$$
$$MR(Q) = 800 - 14Q$$

$$TC(Q) = 2Q^3 - Q^2 + 80Q + 150$$
$$MC(Q) = 6Q^2 - 2Q + 80$$

$$MR(Q) = MC(Q)$$

$$800 - 14Q = 6Q^2 - 2Q + 80$$
$$6Q^2 + 12Q - 720 = 0$$
$$6(Q - 10)(Q + 12) = 0$$

$$Q^* = 10 \text{ and } Q^* = -12$$

$Q^* = -12$ is not a feasible solution and if you check your second order conditions you will see that it is a relative minimum.

At $Q^* = 10$ profits are 4,450

Example 2.8f   **for the following cost function, find where ATC is minimized:**
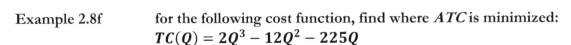
$$TC(Q) = 2Q^3 - 12Q^2 - 225Q$$

Example 2.8f for the following cost function, find where ATC is minimized: $TC(Q) = 2Q^3 - 12Q^2 - 225Q$

Step 1: We are given Total Cost, we need to find Average Total Cost $ATC = \frac{TC}{Q}$

$$TC(Q) = 2Q^2 - 12Q + 225$$

Step 2: Optimize the function by taking first derivative and set it equal to 0

$$TC'(Q) = 4Q - 12 = 0$$
$$Q^* = 3$$

Step 3: Show it is a relative min by taking second derivative

$$TC''(Q) = 4 > 0 \qquad \text{so it is a minimum}$$

You operate a small business that designs websites. Currently you create 15 websites per month and you charge $200 per website. You are thinking about raising your price, but you know that if you raise the price you will get fewer customers. If your price goes up and the number of customers goes down, does that mean you will make less money?

This question can be answered using the Price Elasticity of Demand, denoted with the greek symbol ε. Below is the equation that is used to calculate the price elasticity of demand.

$$\varepsilon_D = \frac{\%\Delta Q}{\%P}$$

*Note: Sometimes you might wonder which goes on bottom, price or quantity. An easy way to remember this is to think of all the econ professors at SUU, Price is the lowest rated. Which makes price go on the bottom of the ratio.

There is a clean interpretation, ε_D is the percent change in quantity for a percent change in price. For example, if $\varepsilon_D = -\frac{1}{2}$, then that means if price increases by 1 percent, quantity will decrease by ½ of a percent. Or if $\varepsilon_D = -2.1$, then a 1 percent increase in price will lead to a 2.1 percent decrease in quantity. More generally, ε_D measures the sensitivity of the demand to changes in prices.

The Elasticity of Demand will fall into three categories:

$|\varepsilon_D| < 1$	**Inelastic**	**Consumers are not price sensitive**
$|\varepsilon_D| = 1$	Unit Elastic	
$|\varepsilon_D| > 1$	Elastic	Consumers are price sensitive

We use the absolute value because ε_D will always be negative. That is because of the law of demand. If price goes up, quantity goes down or if price goes down, quantity goes up. Because P and Q move in opposite directions, elasticity will always be negative.

If a good is inelastic, then that means a 1 percent change in price, leads to a less than 1 percent change in quantity. The following are examples of inelastic goods:

Good	Elasticity	Interpretation
Gasoline	$\varepsilon_D = -.2$	a 10 percent increase in price of gasoline leads to a 2 percent decrease in quantity
Rice	$\varepsilon_D = -0.5$	A 10 percent increase in the price of rice leads to a 5 percent decrease in quantity

Housing	$\varepsilon_D = -0.7$	A 10 percent increase in the price of houses leads to a 7 percent decrease in quantity

If a good is elastic, then a 1 percent increase in price leads to a great that 1 percent decrease in quantity. The following are examples of elastic goods:

Good	Elasticity	Interpretation
Beef	$\varepsilon_D = -1.6$	a 10 percent increase in price of beef leads to a 16 percent decrease in quantity
Restaurant Meals	$\varepsilon_D = -2.3$	A 10 percent increase in the price of restaurant meals leads to a 23 percent decrease in quantity
Mountain Dew	$\varepsilon_D = -4.4$	A 10 percent increase in the price of mountain dew leads to a 44 percent decrease in quantity

To bring this back to the scenario of whether you should increase the price you charge for creating websites. Total revenue is equal to price times quantity. Again, if price goes up, quantity goes down. If price goes up by a lot and quantity goes down by just a little, then total revenue would increase (this just described an inelastic good). By using elasticity we can now get to the punchline:

Type of Good	What happens to Total Revenue when prices increase?
Elastic Good	Total Revenue Decreases
Inelastic Good	Total Revenue Increases

Now let's calculate the price elasticity of demand. We will start with the base equation:

$\varepsilon_D = \frac{\%\Delta Q}{\%P}$ we can rewrite the percent change in the following way

$\varepsilon_D = \frac{\Delta Q / Q}{\Delta P / P}$ in principles of micro you may have written this $\frac{(Q_2 - Q_1)}{Q_1}$

But here we will reorganize the terms slightly different

$\varepsilon_D = \frac{\Delta Q}{\Delta P} * \frac{P}{Q}$ the first term, change of Q for a change of P, can be replaced with a derivative

$\varepsilon_D = \frac{dQ}{dP} * \frac{P}{Q}$ So to find the elasticity of demand, you take the derivative of Quantity with respect to Price, and then multiple by Price divided by Quantity.

$$\varepsilon_D = \frac{\%\Delta Q}{\%P} = \frac{dQ}{dP} * \frac{P}{Q}$$

Example 2.9a Given the Demand Equation, $Q = 20 - \frac{1}{5}P$, calculate the price elasticity of demand and the following points.

    (a) $Q = 4$
    (b) $Q = 10$
    (c) $Q = 15$

Solutions to Example 2.9a

$$\varepsilon_D = \frac{dQ}{dP} * \frac{P}{Q}$$

$$\frac{dQ}{dP} = Q'(P) = -\frac{1}{5}$$

This will be the same for all subparts, now we just need to find the P,Q points and plug them into the equation.

(a) $\qquad Q = 4 \qquad 4 = 20 - \frac{1}{5}P \rightarrow P = 80$

$$\varepsilon_D = \frac{dQ}{dP} * \frac{P}{Q} = -\frac{1}{5} * \frac{80}{4} = -4$$

(b) $\qquad Q = 10 \qquad 10 = 20 - \frac{1}{5}P \rightarrow P = 50$

$$\varepsilon_D = \frac{dQ}{dP} * \frac{P}{Q} = -\frac{1}{5} * \frac{50}{10} = -1$$

(c) $\qquad \mathbf{Q = 15} \qquad\qquad 15 = 20 - \frac{1}{5}P \rightarrow P = 25$

$$\varepsilon_D = \frac{dQ}{dP} * \frac{P}{Q} = -\frac{1}{5} * \frac{25}{15} = -\frac{1}{3}$$

Example 2.9b Given the equation $Q = 80 - 2P$ (where price is measured in dollars, what is the elasticity of demand when Price is \$10 and quantity is 60?

Example 2.9c Building off of the example in 2.8b, instead of measuring price in dollars, let's measure price in cents. This changes the demand equation to the following:

$$Q = 80 - 0.02P$$

Does the elasticity of demand change when the units change?

Solution Example 2.9b

$$\varepsilon_D = \frac{dQ}{dP} * \frac{P}{Q} = -2 * \frac{10}{60} = -.33$$

Solution Example 2.9c

Here we will use the same equation, except that our unity changed. So now, instead of price=$10, it is now price=1,000 cents. Quantity is still the same.

$$\varepsilon_D = \frac{dQ}{dP} * \frac{P}{Q} = -.02 * \frac{1,000}{60} = -.33$$

And it is the same elasticity of demand. So it does not matter what units you measure price or quantity, elasticity of demand at a given point of the demand curve will be the same.

Example 2.9d   Consider the following inverse demand function, $P = 50 - 2Q$
   (a)   Find elasticity of demand when $P = 10$
   (b)   Interpret elasticity at $P = 10$
   (c)   When charging a price of 10, what can the firm do to increase revenue?
   (d)   What happens to demand when price falls by 15%?

Solution Example 2.9d

(a) $\varepsilon_D = \dfrac{dQ}{dP} * \dfrac{P}{Q}$ Notice that the derivative is Q with respect to P, so we cannot use the inverse demand function, the one given in the problem. We need to rewrite it to the demand

$$P = 50 - 2Q \rightarrow Q = 25 - \frac{1}{2}P$$

Now we can apply the equation
$$\varepsilon_D = \frac{dQ}{dP} * \frac{P}{Q} = -\frac{1}{2} * \frac{10}{20} = -.25$$

(b)   If price increases by 1 percent quantity will decrease by ¼ of a percent. Or you could say, a 10 percent increase in price leads to a 2.5 percent decrease in quantity.

(c)   Because $|\varepsilon_D| < 1$, the good is inelastic (consumers are not price sensitive). So an increase in price will lead to an increase in total revenue.

(d)   If the price drops by 15 percent, then quantity will increase by 3.75 percent (15*.25)

Consider the following inverse demand equation: $P = 150 - 10Q$. We can use that to calculate and graph out a total revenue function. The graph is shown below:

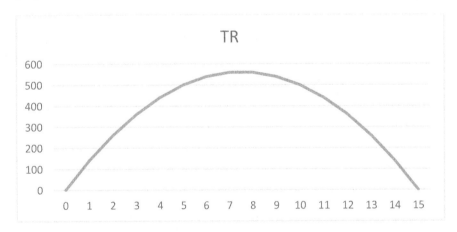

At $Q = 10,$ if you decrease the quantity produced, total revenues would increase. So how do you decrease quantity? You increase the price. If increasing the price leads to higher revenues then it would suggest that the at $Q = 10$, the good is inelastic.

Example 2.9e   Show that at $Q = 10$, the price elasticity of demand is inelastic for the example above.

Example 2.9f   Calculate the price elasticity of demand at the point which maximizes total revenue of the example above.

Solution Example 2.9e

The inverse demand equation is given, so we need to re-write it as the demand equation. $Q = 15 - \frac{1}{10Q}$

We can now apply the elasticity equation: $\varepsilon_D = -\frac{1}{10} * \frac{50}{10} = -\frac{1}{2}$

$|\varepsilon_D| = \frac{1}{2} < 1$ so this is indeed inelastic, as raising the price would reduce the quantity and have a resulting effect of increasing total revenues.

Solution Example 2.9f

First, let's find the point that maximizes total revenue
$P = 150 - 10Q$
$TR = 150Q - 10Q^2$
$TR'(Q) = 150 - 20Q$
$Q^* = 7.5$
At that point, $P^* = 75$

$\varepsilon_D = -\frac{1}{10} * \frac{75}{7.5} = -1$

So at this point, we are at unit elasticity. Meaning that if you increase or lower price, total revenue will decrease.
At the revenue maximizing quantity and price, elasticity of demand is -1

See Videos: https://www.youtube.com/watch?v=faSxhJxc1eQ
https://www.youtube.com/watch?v=fDKmfRsJqtc

Example 2.9g   **A firm is currently selling its product at a price of $12 per unit. It knows that, at this price, the own-price elasticity of demand is -1.5. By how much should it change price to increase sales volume by 5%?**

Solution Example 2.9g

$$\varepsilon_D = -1.5 = \frac{\%\Delta Q}{\%\Delta P}$$

We know that we want to increase sales volume by 5%, or increase Q by 5%

$$\varepsilon_D = -1.5 = \frac{5}{\%\Delta P} \rightarrow \%\Delta P = -3.33$$

So price needs to decrease by 3.33%, which means price goes from $12 to $11.60

See Videos: https://www.youtube.com/watch?v=Y8w6W-bvRQM

Chapter 3
Multivariate Calculus

Why would anyone want to use multivariate calculus?

Because they want to make money. Now you might think that answer to be too simple, so let me make it a little more complex for you. If you buy that simple answer, just skip ahead to learn how to use multivariate calculus.

Your ambition drives you to be a manager of the local Costa Vida (let's be honest, if you have ever lived in Cedar City, you know that Costa is way better than Café Rio. In other cities this may not be true, but here in the land of the Juniper trees, it is absolutely the truth.). You can advertise those delicious smothered burritos or your cilantro lime covered pulled pork salad. Which one should you advertise?

And now you know why you would want to use multivariate calculus. You have two things you can choose that contribute to your goal of making money. You can use the demand of burritos and the demand for salads to jointly estimate how you should set your prices. This is important because if a customer comes into the restaurant, and the price of burritos is half of that as a salad, it will affect the sales of both products.

In any setting where there are multiple interrelated choices, multivariate regression can be used to make optimal choices.

Chapter 3.1 First Partial Derivatives

Let's go back to the base example: $y = mx + b$. In this example m is the slope or $\frac{\Delta y}{\Delta x}$. The derivative is the $\frac{\Delta y}{\Delta x}$ at a given point on a function. We changed the notation a little and said the derivative was $\frac{df(x)}{dx}$ or $f'(x)$.

We can build on this and start with a function that has two variables: $f(x_1, x_2)$. When we take a derivative now, what we are asking is how does the function change when one of the variables changes. They key here is only one variable will change, the other variable is not going to change, or as we will say in this class, be held constant.

For example, let's look at the demand of hot dog buns (Q_B). What is going to effect the number of hot dog buns you buy, two things: price of hot dog buns (P_B) and the price of the hot dogs (P_D). A simple function can be written to show the relationship between the price of both items and the quantity demanded:

$$Q_B = 20 - 2P_B - \frac{1}{2}P_D$$

What a derivative will do in this case is to answer the question, holding constant the price of hot dogs, what happens to the demand of buns when the price of buns increases? We call that the first partial derivative with respect to the price of buns. We can write that out with the following notation:

$\frac{\partial Q_B(P_B, P_D)}{\partial P_B}$ We use the curly d (∂) to indicate that there are more than one variable. This notation is interpreted as the change in Q_B when the variable P_B changes, or what happens to the quantity of buns when the price of buns changes.

Instead if we wanted to see what happens to the quantity of buns when the price of hot dogs changes, we would want to hold the price of buns fixed, and let the price of hot dogs change:
$\frac{\partial Q_B(P_B, P_D)}{\partial P_D}$

Now let's build out generic equations to show what a first partial derivative does.

Consider the function with two variables, x and y, $f(x, y)$

The formal definition of a partial derivative is as follows:

$$Slope\ of\ Tangent\ when\ x\ changes = \lim_{\Delta x \to 0} \frac{f(x+\Delta x, y) - f(x,y)}{\Delta x}$$

$$Slope\ of\ Tangent\ when\ y\ changes = \lim_{\Delta y \to 0} \frac{f(x, y+\Delta y) - f(x,y)}{\Delta y}$$

Informally, we follow the same rules as before. When we are taking the derivative with respect to x, we hold y as a constant, that means treat it as any other number.

For example, $f(x,y) = 3xy^2$

How would we take the first partial derivatives with respect to y and x?

Let's start with x, we can write the partial derivative two ways, $\frac{\partial f(x,y)}{\partial x}$ or $f_x(x,y)$

Here we treat y as a constant, so we could re-write the function in the following way:

$$f(x,y) = (3y^2)x$$

Here $3y^2$ is just some number because we are holding y constant, so to take the derivative you would use the linear rule and get

$$f_x = 3y^2$$

Now let's take the derivative with respect to y, and you can re-write the function as follows:

$$f(x,y) = (3x)y^2$$

We would treat $3x$ as the constant k, and use the power rule:

$$f_y = 2 * 3x * y^{2-1} = 6xy$$

And there you have it, that is who you can take first partial derivatives.

See Video: https://www.youtube.com/watch?v=Z_muixmYdUs

Example 3.1a   Given the multivariate function $f(x, y) = 3x^2 + 18x - 2y + 4y^2$ find the first partial derivatives with respect to x and y

Example 3.1b   Given the multivariate function $f(x, y) = -2x^2 + 3xy - 8y^2 - 32$ find $\frac{\partial f(x,y)}{\partial x}$ and $\frac{\partial f(x,y)}{\partial y}$

Example 3.1c   Given the function $f(x, y) = -4x^2y^2 - 3x + 4y^3$, find both first partial derivatives

Example 3.1d   Given the function $f(x, y) = 4x^3 - 2x^2 - 3xy^2$, find f_x *and* f_y

Solutions Example 3.1a

$f(x, y) = 3x^2 + 18x - 2y + 4y^2$

$\frac{df(x,y)}{dx} = f_x = 6x + 18 - 0 + 0$

$\frac{df(x,y)}{dy} = f_y = 0 + 0 - 2 + 8y$

Solutions Example 3.1b

$\frac{df(x,y)}{dx} = -4x + 3y$

$\frac{df(x,y)}{dy} = 3x - 16y$

Solutions Example 3.1c

$\frac{df(x,y)}{dx} = -8xy^2 - 3$

$\frac{df(x,y)}{dy} = -8x^2y + 12y^2$

Solutions Example 3.1d

$\frac{df(x,y)}{dx} = 12x^2 - 4x - 3y^2$

$\frac{df(x,y)}{dy} = -6xy$

Chapter 3.2   Second Partial Derivatives

Similar to when there is one variable, we can take second derivatives when we have two variables. The notation is similar and is shown below.

The second derivative with respect to x can be shown in the following way:

$$f_{xx} = \frac{\partial}{\partial x}\left[\frac{\partial f(x,y)}{\partial x}\right] = \frac{\partial^2 f(x,y)}{\partial x^2}$$

This means that we start inside the bracket, we first take the partial derivative with respect to x, and then take the partial derivative a second time with respect to x.

The second derivative with respect to y can be shown in the following way:

$$f_{yy} = \frac{\partial}{\partial y}\left[\frac{\partial f(x,y)}{\partial y}\right] = \frac{\partial^2 f(x,y)}{\partial y^2}$$

Let's do an example together. We have the function $f(x,y) = 3x^2 + 18x - 2y + 4y^2$

Let's take the partial derivative with respect to x.
$$\frac{df(x,y)}{dx} = f_x = 6x + 18 - 0 + 0$$

Now let's take the derivative of the first derivative with respect to x, and we get the following:
$$\frac{d^2 f(x,y)}{dx^2} = f_{xx} = 6$$

We can do the same thing for y, take the first partial derivative
$$\frac{df(x,y)}{dy} = f_y = 0 + 0 - 2 + 8y$$

Take the derivative of the first derivative function with respect to y
$$\frac{d^2 f(x,y)}{dy^2} = f_{yy} = 8$$

Example 3.2a Find the second partial derivatives for each of the functions:

(a) $f(x,y) = -2x^2 + 3xy - 8y^2 - 32$

(b) $f(x,y) = -4x^2y^2 - 3x + 4y^3$

(a) $f(x, y) = -2x^2 + 3xy - 8y^2 - 32$

$\dfrac{df(x,y)}{dx} = -4x + 3y$ 　　　　　　　　$\dfrac{df(x,y)}{dy} = 3x - 16y$

$\dfrac{d^2f(x,y)}{dx^2} = -4$ 　　　　　　　　$\dfrac{d^2f(x,y)}{dy^2} = -16$

(b) $f(x, y) = -4x^2y^2 - 3x + 4y^3$

$\dfrac{df(x,y)}{dx} = -8xy^2 - 3$ 　　　　　　$\dfrac{df(x,y)}{dy} = -8x^2y + 12y^2$

$\dfrac{d^2f(x,y)}{dx^2} = -8y^2$ 　　　　　　　$\dfrac{d^2f(x,y)}{dy^2} = -8x^2 + 24y$

Cross Partial Derivatives

In addition to the second partial derivatives with respect to x and y, we can also take the cross partial derivatives. This means that we take the derivative first with respect to x and then we take the derivative with respect to y (or vice versa, y first then x).

We represent the cross partial derivatives in the following way:

$$f_{xy} = \frac{\partial}{\partial y}\left[\frac{\partial f(x,y)}{\partial x}\right] = \frac{\partial^2 f(x,y)}{\partial y \partial x} \qquad\qquad f_{yx} = \frac{\partial}{\partial x}\left[\frac{\partial f(x,y)}{\partial y}\right] = \frac{\partial^2 f(x,y)}{\partial x \partial y}$$

Let's try this with the following function: $f(x, y) = 3x^2 + 18xy - 2y^2 + 4y^3$

$f_x = 6x + 18y$ 　　　　　　$f_y = 18x - 4y + 12y^2$
$f_{xy} = 18$ 　　　　　　　　$f_{yx} = 18$

Will it always be the case that $f_{xy} = f_{yx}$? Yes it will, this is called Young's Theorem, and it states that $f_{xy} = f_{yx}$. So the order in which you take the cross partial derivatives does not matter.

Example 3.2b For the following functions, find the two second order derivatives and the cross partial derivative.

(a) $f(x, y) = -2x^2 + 3xy - 8y^2 - 32$

(b) $f(x, y) = -4x^2y^2 - 3x + 4y^3$

Solution Example 3.2b

(a)
$$f(x, y) = -2x^2 + 3xy - 8y^2 - 32$$

$$\frac{df(x,y)}{dx} = -4x + 3y \qquad\qquad \frac{df(x,y)}{dy} = 3x - 16y$$

$$\frac{d^2f(x,y)}{dx^2} = -4 \qquad\qquad \frac{d^2f(x,y)}{dy^2} = -16$$

$$\frac{d^2f(x,y)}{dxdy} = 3 \qquad\qquad \frac{d^2f(x,y)}{dydx} = 3$$

(b)
$$f(x, y) = -4x^2y^2 - 3x + 4y^3$$

$$\frac{df(x,y)}{dx} = -8xy^2 - 3 \qquad\qquad \frac{df(x,y)}{dy} = -8x^2y + 12y^2$$

$$\frac{d^2f(x,y)}{dx^2} = -8y^2 \qquad\qquad \frac{d^2f(x,y)}{dy^2} = -8x^2 + 24y$$

$$\frac{d^2f(x,y)}{dxdy} = -16xy \qquad\qquad \frac{d^2f(x,y)}{dydx} = -16xy$$

Chapter 3.3 Optimization of Multivariable Functions

With just one variable, it is easy to see what we mean by optimization. It is simply finding the top of curve, a 2-dimensional curve. Simply the high or low point of a parabola.

With two variables, which is the majority of what we will do in this chapter, when we are optimizing, we are finding the top of a hill or the bottom of the valley. In fact, Marvin Gaye and Tammi Terrill sang all about this in they rendition of *Ain't No Mountain High Enough* (Link).

Similar to before, we follow the same pattern:

(1) Take the first derivatives
(2) Set them both equal to 0
(3) Solve for the optimal value of x and y
(4) Check the second order condition to show if it is a relative minimum or relative maximum.

Here is a summary of the rule of maximum and minimum

	Maximum	Minimum
First order condition	$f_x = 0$ $f_y = 0$	$f_x = 0$ $f_y = 0$
Second order condition	$f_{xx} < 0$ $f_{yy} < 0$ $(f_{xx})(f_{yy}) > f_{xy}^2$	$f_{xx} > 0$ $f_{yy} > 0$ $(f_{xx})(f_{yy}) > f_{xy}^2$

Focusing on the second order conditions, if the second partial derivatives are less than zero (frowny face) then it is likely we have a relative min, but there is still one more condition that needs to be met.

The last part of the second order condition is that the product of the second derivatives is greater than the cross partial squared, $(f_{xx})(f_{yy}) > f_{xy}^2$. To show that a point is a relative maximum, it is necessary to show that all three equations hold for the second order conditions.

Let's work through an example together. Consider the function

$$f(x) = 3x^2 + 2x + 4y^2 - 8y$$

To find the x,y values that optimize the function, we take the first derivates (plural) and set them equal to zero.

$$f_x = 6x + 2 = 0 \qquad\qquad x^* = -\frac{1}{3}$$
$$f_y = 8y - 8 = 0 \qquad\qquad y^* = 1$$

Now to show that this point is a relative max or min we need to check the second order conditions.

$$f_{xx} = 6 > 0$$
$$f_{yy} = 8 > 0$$

Now for the third one

$$f_{xy} = 0 \quad \text{since } f_x \text{ does not have the y variable in the function}$$
$$(f_{xx})(f_{yy}) > f_{xy}^2 \qquad\qquad (6)(8) > 0^2$$

All three parts of the second order condition are satisfied so, in this case, we have a relative minimum.

Example 3.3a   **Given the following equation, find the point that optimizes the function and show if it is a relative max or min.**

$$f(x,y) = -x^2 + 16x + 18y - \frac{3}{2}y^2 + 15$$

Solution Example 3.3a

First order conditions
$f_x = -2x + 16 = 0$ $\qquad x^* = 8$
$f_y = 18 - 3y = 0$ $\qquad y^* = 6$

Second order conditions
$f_{xx} = -2 < 0$
$f_{yy} = -3 < 0$
$f_{xy} = 0$
$(-2)(-3) > 0$
Therefore, it is a relative maximum

Example 3.3b   **Given the following equation, find the point that optimizes the function and show if it is a relative max or min.**

$$f(x, y) = -7x^2 + 88x - 6xy + 42y - 2y^2 + 4$$

Solution Example 3.3b

$f_x = -14x + 88 - 6y = 0$

$f_y = -6x + 42 - 4y = 0$

Now we have a system of equations, that is we have two unknowns (x,y) and two equations. There are several ways to solve this:

1. Solve one equation for a variable and plug it into the other equation. Let's use the first equation and solve for y

$6y = -14x + 88$

$y = \frac{-14x+88}{6}$ plug this into the second equation

$-6x + 42 - 4\left[\frac{-14x+88}{6}\right] = 0$ multiply everything by 6 to get rid of the 6 in the denominator

$-36x + 252 + 56x - 352 = 0$

$100 = 20x$

$x^* = 5$ now plug this into either equation to solve for y

$-6(5) + 42 - 4y = 0$

$y^* = 3$

2. Another way is to use excel and set this up in solver.

	A	B
1	x	y
2		
3	fx	88
4	fy	=-6*A2+42-4*B2

Set B2=0 as objective and then add a constraint that B4=0, then solve

$x^* = 5$ and $y^* = 3$

Second order conditions

$f_{xx} = -14 < 0$

$f_{yy} = -4 < 0$

$f_{xy} = -6$

$(-14)(-4) > (-6)^2$

We have a relative minimum

See Video: https://www.youtube.com/watch?v=RRbo8BXJ7Rw

Example 3.3c   Given the following equation, find the point that optimizes the function and show if it is a relative max or min.

$$f(x, y) = -2x^2 + 14x - 76xy + 24y - 2y^2 + 4$$

Solution Example 3.3c

First order conditions
$$f_x = -4x + 14 - 76y = 0$$
$$f_y = -76x + 24 - 4y = 0$$

Set up in solver
$$x^* = 0.31 \quad \text{and} \quad y^* = 0.17$$

Second order conditions
$$f_{xx} = -4 < 0$$
$$f_{yy} = -4 < 0$$
$$f_{xy} = -76$$
$$(-4)(-4) < (-76)^2 \qquad \text{which is not the condition}$$

Therefore, we do not have a relative max or min.

Using www.wolframalpha.com, we can graph out this function (just copy and paste the function $f(x, y)$ into the search bar in the website. It will give you a graphical view, which may or may not be helpful.

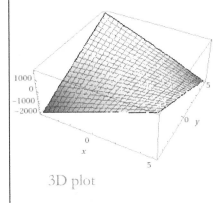

3D plot

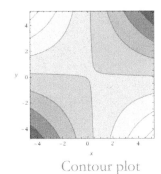

Contour plot

What these figures show is that there is not a single point that optimizes the function, but several points that due. When all three second order conditions are not met, it does not mean the function does not have a minimum, it may mean that there is not only one single point at which the function is minimized.

Example 3.3d   Find the profit-maximizing prices and outputs for the multi-product monopolist with the following demand and cost functions. Find maximum profit.

$$P_x = 92 - 2x \qquad P_y = 176 - 5y$$
$$TC(x, y) = 3x^2 + xy + 2y^2 + 424$$

Solution Example 3.3d

To solve this one, let's go back to the equation that we have for TR

$TR = PQ$

In this case, we have two products so

$TR(x, y) = P_x x + P_y y$
$= (92 - 2x)x + (176 - 5y)y$

Now we look at $profits = TR - TC$

We can set this all up in Excel (double click on the picture below to see the functions in each cell)

x	y			
Px	Py			
92	176			
TR(x)	TR(y)	TR(x,y)	TC(x,y)	Profits
0	0	0	424	-424

Solution is $x^* = 8 \; and \; y^* = 12$

See video: https://www.youtube.com/watch?v=N9O52xXX-tU

Optimization problems are useful, but even more useful are constrained optimization problems. For example, your marketing department comes to you and says, increase our budge and we can increase sales. Then your research and development department interjects and says a little more development will make your product so superior that sales will increase. Then some random dude in the corner says he knows a guy who knows a guy, and if you give him some money he can increase sales.

You want your sales to increase, so why not give your marketing department the money they asked for and your R&D team their requested funds? (A good boss would ignore that random dude in the corner.) That is because you have a budget and while you would like to maximize your sales, you are constrained with how much you can spend. We can incorporate these constraints in optimization problems.

Consider the following equation $sales(x, y) = -x^2 + 16x + 18y - \frac{3}{2}y^2 + 15$ where x are dollars given to marketing and y are dollars give to R&D. Here dollars are measured in millions and you only have $10 million dollars in your budget.

If you optimize the function (see example 3.3a) you know that the optimal amount to increase sales would be to give marketing $8 million and R&D $6 million. But you don't have $14 million to give, so how do you do that.

We can write out an equation that optimizes a function subject to a constraint in the following way:

$$\max sales(x, y) = -x^2 + 16x + 18y - \frac{3}{2}y^2 + 15$$
$$subject\ to \quad x + y \leq 10$$

You want to spend all of your budget, since each dollar spent will increase sales, so the constraint will be binding, which means
$$x + y = 10$$

You can rewrite the budget to equal 0 in the following way
$$10 - x - y = 0$$

We do that because a mathematician, Joseph-Louis Lagrange, said that you add 0 to a function, it does not change that function. For example, $f(x) = 5x$ if you add a zero, all you get is $f(x) = 5x + 0$ which doesn't change the function at all. And that is what we are going to do here. When we add a 0 term to the function we call this a Lagrangian Equation.[1]

Joseph Louis Lagrange (1736-1813) His birth name was Guiseppe Luigi Lagrangia. In 1808, Napoleon made him a Grand Officer of the Legion of Honour. He has a moon crater named after him.

We write a Lagrange equation in the following way:

$$\mathcal{L} = f(x, y) + \lambda(constraint = 0)$$

---

[1] If you are considering names for your children, I encourage you to consider Lagrange. That name will not be shared with any other child in the class.

See videos: https://www.youtube.com/watch?v=_khfskxatQE
https://www.youtube.com/watch?v=MfFC2keSQrQ

In our specific example, we would write it out in the following way:

$$\mathcal{L} = \left(-x^2 + 16x + 18y - \frac{3}{2}y^2 + 15\right) + \lambda(10 - x - y)$$

This first part is the original function; then we add a λ multiplied by the constraint. Lambda (λ), is a number (we don't know what it is yet) that is called the Lagrange multiplier. We can do that because the next term is the constraint, which equals zero. And we all know that λ times zero is zero.

If we wanted to optimize this function, we would apply the same rules of the first order conditions

$$f_x = -2x + 16 - \lambda = 0$$
$$f_y = 18 - 3y - \lambda = 0$$

Notice that the first order conditions take into account the Lagrange multiplier (λ). We now have two equations and three variables, which cannot be solved. So we need to take one more first derivative, this time with respect to λ:

$$f_\lambda = 10 - x - y = 0$$

This equation is the constraint. We would then solve this for $x^*, y^*, and\ \lambda^*$. This is unpleasant to do by hand. Let's do it in solver instead.

We set it up with variables x and y and an objective function (sales).

	A	B	C
1	x	y	
2			
3			
4	sal=-A2^2+16*A2+18*B2-(3/2)*B2^2+15		

We now add a constraint. I will go back to the original equation and add that in

	A	B
1	x	y
2		
3		
4	sales(x,y)	15
5	constraint	
6	LHS	RHS
7	=A2+B2	10

We now can turn to solver, where the objective is to maximize sales (B4), by changing x and y (A2:B2). We can add a constraint such that the Left Hand Side (LHS) is less than or equal to the Right Hand Side (RHS) or $A7 \leq B7$

Then click solve and voilá, we have our answer.

$$x^* = 10 \; and \; y^* = 0$$

Meaning that we give our entire budget to marketing and nothing to R&D, this will cause our sales to be the highest.

A couple of things about Lagrange Multiplier.

- There is an important interpretation of the Lagrange multiplier. λ is interpreted as the change in the objective function for a change in the constraint.
  In the previous example, the Lagrange multiplier would be interpreted as the change in sales for a change in the budget constraint. You could use this number to estimate how much sales would increase if you increased your budget by a little amount. #veryuseful

- You do not need to include it as a variable when you set up the problem in Excel. It is secretly hiding behind the scenes when you include a constraint.

- Excel will calculate the Lagrange multiplier if you run a sensitivity report. After you click Solve in Solver, your computer will make a sound and open a new window that looks like this:

Under Reports, click on Sensitivity, it should turn to blue highlights, then click OK. This will create a new worksheet called Sensitivity Report 1. If you click on that, then it will show you a report with the Lagrange Multiplier!!!!

	Constraints			
11				
12	Constraints			
13			Final	Lagrange
14	Cell	Name	Value	Multiplier
15	$A$7	LHS	10	36.00001216

With this information, if you were to increase the budget by 1 (or $1 million dollars) sales would increase by 36. This can then be used to make a decision as to whether an increase of sales of 36 will create more revenue that the $1 million cost.

- The Lagrange multiplier is not your friend, but a business partner that is there to help you make good business decisions. #betterthanafriend

Example 3.4a   What is the value of x and y that solves the following constrained optimization problem? Calculate the Lagrange multiplier.

Maximize $f(x, y) = 120x - 4x^2 + 2xy - 3y^2 + 96y - 102$
Subject to $x + 3y \leq 69$

Solution Example 3.4a

The Lagrangian would be:
$$\mathcal{L} = 120x - 4x^2 + 2xy - 3y^2 + 96y - 102 + \lambda(69 - x - 3y)$$

To set it up in Excel it would look like this:

x	y	
f(x,y)	=120*A2-4*A2^2+2*A2*B2-3*B2^2+96*B2-102	
LHS		RHS
=A2+3*B2	<=	69

Then go to Solver

Click solve and the result should be
$$x^* = 18 \ and \ y^* = 17$$

Run the Sensitivity Report to find that the Lagrange multiplier is

12	Constraints			
13			Final	Lagrange
14	Cell	Name	Value	Multiplier
15	$A$4	x	69	9.999982178

Rounded to 2 decimal places, $\lambda^* = 10$

See the Video: https://www.youtube.com/watch?v=0SglVagkAUU

119

Example 3.4b   What are the values of x and y that minimize this constrained
                optimization problem? Calculate the Lagrange multiplier.

    Minimize $f(x, y) = 5x^2 - 2xy + 8y^2$
        Subject to $x + y \geq 60$

Example 3.4c   A company is under contract to deliver 77 units of two products, x and
                y, in any combination. Given the following cost function, find the
                combination that minimizes the cost of fulfilling the contract.

    $TC(x, y) = 7x^2 - 2xy + 5y^2 + 64$

Example 3.4d   A retail store estimated the following market response function giving
                sales (s) as a function of the number of advertisements in circulars (x)
                and the number of advertisements in newspapers (y):
    $s(x, y) = 420x - 2x^2 - 3xy - 5y^2 + 640y + 1725$
                Find the optimal advertising plan given an advertising budget of $180
                per period, and assuming the cost is $1 per ad for circulars and $4 per
                ad for newspapers. Also, use the Lagrange multiplier to estimate the
                effect on sales of a $1 increase in the advertising budget.

Solution Example 3.4b

To solve

	A	B	C
1	x	y	
2			
3	f(x,y)	0	
4	LHS		RHS
5	0	>=	60
6			
7			
8			
9			
10			
11			

Solver Parameters

Set Objective: $BS3

To: ○ Max ● Min ○ Value Of: 0

By Changing Variable Cells:

$A$2:$B$2

Subject to the Constraints:

$A$5 >= $C$5   Add

                      Change

$x^* = 36$ and $y^* = 24$

$\lambda^* = 312$

see video: https://www.youtube.com/watch?v=x3BGsI7oP6M

Solution Example 3.4c

Set up constrained optimization problem:

$Minimize\ TC(x,y) = 7x^2 - 2xy + 5y^2 + 64$

s.t $x + y \leq 77$

$x^* = 33$ and $y^* = 44$ and $\lambda^* = 374$

See the video: https://www.youtube.com/watch?v=EubSBVjlZxY

Solution Example 3.4d

Set up constrained optimization problem

$Max\ sales = 420x - 2x^2 - 3xy - 5y^2 + 640y + 1725$

s.t. $x + 4y \leq 180$

$x^* = 76$ and $y^* = 26$

$\lambda^* = 38$ which means that an increase in the budget of \$1 would increase slates by 38.

Example 3.4e   Suppose a firm has a production function (called a "Cobb-Douglas" production function) given by

$$Q = 1.5K^{0.6}L^{0.4}$$

Assume the budget is \$960, the price of capital (*K*) is $P_K = \$6$, and the price of labor (*L*) is $P_L = \$2$. Determine the amounts labor and capital that maximize output. Estimate the benefit of having an additional dollar in the budget.

Solution Example 3.4e

Set up constrained optimization

Maximize $Q = 1.5K^{0.6}L^{0.4}$
    s.t. $6K + 2L \le 960$

Set it up in Excel

$K^* = 96$ and $L^* = 192$

*note: if K and L cells are blank when you run solver, you will get answers of 0 and 0. So just put any number into the cells for K and L and then run solver again.

$\lambda^* = .20$

So increasing the budget by \$1 will increase quantity by .2. To get a full unit of additional output it will take \$5.

See video https://www.youtube.com/watch?v=4RX-FRfjgrY

This section is for information, but will not be evaluated or assessed in this course

Integration is reversing the process of differentiation. We ask ourselves, what is the function of which I have to take the derivative to find this function? This is why it is sometimes called anti-differentiation.

The notation for integral is $\int$

What is the integral of the following function?
$\int 2x \, dx$

To answer this, we ask, what is the function that we take the derivative of in order to get 2x? The *dx* is the notation to identify the variable.

The function would be x^2. Because we would bring down the two and subtract one from the exponent.

But we need to add one more thing. If the original function was $x^2 + 4$, we would get 2x and the derivative of 4 is zero. So anytime we take the derivative, we need to add a number to the end, to account for any constants that are added to the original function. We do this by simply writing + c.

So the answer is: $\int 2x \, dx = x^2 + c$

In general, the rule for integration is as follows:

$$\int kx^n \, dx = \frac{k}{n+1} x^{n+1} + c$$

Example 3.5a Find the integrals of the following functions:

(a) $\int 4x \, dx$

(b) $\int (4x + 3) \, dx$

(c) $\int (15x^2 + 4x + 2) \, dx$

Solutions Example 3.5a

(a) $\int 4x\, dx = 2x^2 + c$

(b) $\int (4x + 3)\, dx = 2x^2 + 3x + c$

(c) $\int (15x^2 + 4x + 2)\, dx = 5x^3 + 2x^2 + 2x + c$

See Video: https://www.youtube.com/watch?v=yK9bGJ1ZS_M

Area under a Curve

- The area under a curve from $x = a$ to $x = b$ can be approximated with

$A = \sum_{i=1}^{n} f(x_i)\, \Delta x_i,$ where $\Delta x = \dfrac{b-a}{n}$

- The approximation becomes better as Δx_i gets smaller and n gets larger.

- The exact area is given by the *definite integral* of $f(x)$ over the interval a to b:

$$\int_a^b f(x)\, dx = \lim_{n \to \infty} \sum_{i=1}^{n} f(x_i)\, \Delta x_i$$

The Fundamental Theorem of Calculus

$$\int_a^b f(x)\, dx = F(x)|_a^b = F(b) - F(a)$$

See Videos: https://www.youtube.com/watch?v=GBtYNlp7jEk

https://www.youtube.com/watch?v=WctRv50TkxQ

Example 3.5b   **Find the integral of the following function**
$\int_{-1}^{3} 2x\, dx$

Solution Example 3.5b

First, find the integral: $(x^2 + c)|^3_{-1}$
Now evaluate it from points 3 to -1: $(3)^2 + c - [(-1)^2 + c] = 9 + c - 1 - c = 8$
Thus, our answer is 8.

Example 3.5c   Find the integral of the following functions:

a) $\int_2^8 4x\, dx$

b) $\int_1^5 (-3x^2 + 8x + 40)dx$

Solutions Example 3.5c

a) $\int_2^8 4x\, dx$

$$= 2(8)^2 + c - 2(2)^2 - c = 120$$

a) $\int_1^5 (-3x^2 + 8x + 40)dx$
$$= [-(5)^3 + 4(5)^2 + 40(5) + c] - [-(-1)^3 + 4(1)^2 + 40(1) + c]$$
$$= [-125 + 100 + 200 + c] - [-1 + 4 + 40 - c]$$
$$= 132$$

Chapter 4
Linear Programming

In the Summer of 1998, Major League Baseball saw a rejuvenation in the game. More fans were coming out to the ballpark than in recent years. Television ratings were sky high. What could have caused this phenomenon?

Roger Maris hit 61 home runs in 1961. Since then, no player had ever hit more than 61 home runs in a season. Yet in the Summer of 1998, two All-Stars were on pace to break that record.

Mark McGwire of the St. Louis Cardinals and Sammy Sosa of the Chicago Cubs were hitting home runs at a greater rate than any player in history.

It was almost as if they were on steroids. It turns out they were on steroids, both of them. And that was one of the contributing factors that lead them to both break the record that year. But don't worry, their record was broken shortly thereafter by another player, Barry Bonds. He also used steroids.

What does this have to do with Linear Programming? Everything!! What we can do with linear programming is to take what we have done with constrained optimization and add some steroids. Not the kind that leads you into a rage, at least I hope not, but we will build upon the principles of constrained optimization and give you the power to do a lot more.

So let's pump you up with knowledge and skills instead of steroids.

Linear programming is the business application of constrained maximization. It deals with different objective functions of the firm, organization or individual and with linear constraints.

Each linear programming example will have three parts
1. The scenario – here is the real world example, written out as you might see it if you lived in the real world
2. Linear Program – here is where you will use linear programming to solve the real world example
3. Implications and Conclusions – what can you do to improve the scenario

Intro to Linear Program Video: https://www.youtube.com/watch?v=onSc_KEa1uM

A linear program can be written out and has three parts. I highly encourage that each of you, as your work on each problem, write out the linear program. Do not skip a step. Those steps are

> 1. Define the variable including units
> 2. Identify the objective function
> 3. Write out each constraint

Let's look at an example together and write out the linear program.

Example 4.1a   **A certain firm makes two models of spas: AS and HL. Each AS model requires 1 pump, 9 hours of labor and 12 feet of tubing; each HL model requires 1 pump, 6 hours of labor and 16 feet of tubing. In a given production period the company is limited to using at most 200 pumps, 1566 hours of labor and 2880 feet of tubing. The profit margin (price minus direct production costs) on AS spas is \$350; the profit margin on HL spas is \$300. The company wants to determine the optimal production plan.**

Step 1: To write out the linear program, we need to first define the variables. The guiding question in defining the variables is what is it that you get to choose? In this case, we do not get to choose pumps, labor, or tubing. They are all features of the different types of spas. What we get to choose are the number of each type of spa to produce.

$$\text{Let} \quad x_1 = number\ of\ AS\ spas\ produced$$
$$x_2 = number\ of\ HL\ spas\ produced$$

Step 2: Identify the objective. Here the scenario mentions that we want to determine the optimal production plan. What does this entail? Maximizing profits of course. The objective function should be a function of the variables defined in step 1. We get \$350 for each AS spa produced, so profits are equal to 350 times the number of AS spas. The same is true for HL spas and can be written in the following manner:

$$\max profits = 350x_1 + 300x_2$$

Step 3: We need to write out each constraint. While we would like to make as many AS spas as possible, since they give us a better profit margin, we are constrained with the amount of pumps, labor, and tubing that we have. Let's focus on pumps, you take the number of pumps required to produce one spa and multiply it by the number of spas produced. This can be represented as the first constraint

Pumps (i) $1x_1 + 1x_2 \leq 200$ there are only 200 pumps available.

The same can be done with labor and tubing

Labor (ii) $9x_1 + 6x_2 \leq 1566$
Tubing (iii) $12x_1 + 16x_2 \leq 2880$

We can now combine all three steps to get the final linear program:

Let $x_1 = $ *number of AS spas produced*
       $x_2 = $ *number of HL spas produced*

$$\max profits = 350x_1 + 300x_2$$
s.t. (i) $1x_1 + 1x_2 \leq 200$
            (ii) $9x_1 + 6x_2 \leq 1566$
            (iii) $12x_1 + 16x_2 \leq 2880$

Now that we have set up the linear program, there are two ways to solve the linear program.
1.   Graphically
2.   With Solver

For this class you will be expected to solve a linear program using both methods. So let's take a look at how to do this graphically first.

To graph this out, we want to rewrite the constraints, such that it looks more like $y = mx + b$. In this case, we will treat the x_2 variable as our y variable and x_1 as our x variable. Thus the constraints can be written the following way:

Pumps: $x_2 \leq 200 - x_1$

Labor: $x_2 \leq 261 - \frac{3}{2}x_1$

Tubing: $x_2 \leq 180 - \frac{3}{4}x_1$

Try to graph out the previous constraints on the graph below:

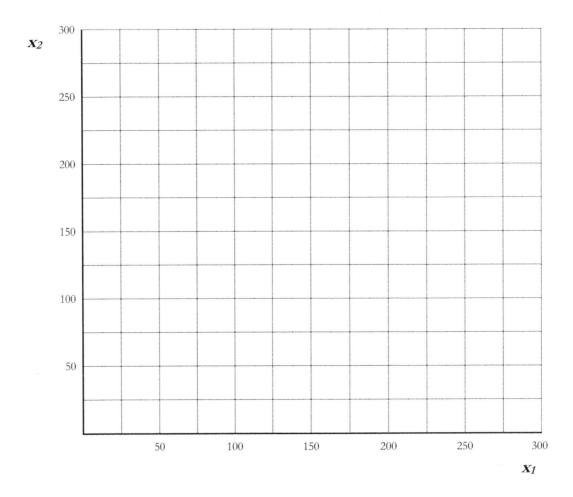

The solution looks like this:

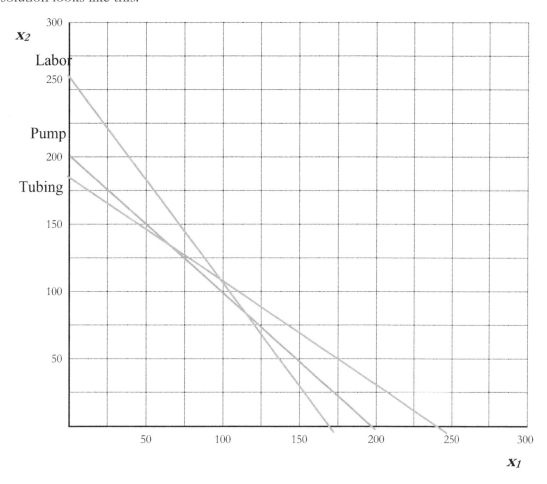

The next step in solving the linear programming is to identify where the possible solutions. We call this the feasible region and contains a set of points that meet the restrictions imposed by the constraints.

Consider if the company produced 50 AS spas and 50 HL spas. Is this feasible? Let's look at each constraint:

> Pumps (i) $1(50) + 1(50) = 100 \leq 200$
> Labor (ii) $9(50) + 6(50) = 750 \leq 1566$
> Tubing (iii) $12(50) + 16(50) = 1400 \leq 2880$

All the constraints hold, meaning that the amount of each input used is below the capacity. Graphically, you can look at the point 50,50 and see that it falls below each of the lines. Since the equations for the constraints used to graph them indicates that $x_2 \leq$ the function, then the feasible region is any point that is less than or equal to all three lines.

In this example, the feasible region starts when the Tubing constraint intersects the y-axis, then moves along the Tubing constraint (the green line), until it intersects with the Pump constraint. Then it moves along that line (the blue line) until the intersection of the Labor and Pump constraint, the feasible region continues down the Labor constraint (orange line) until it reaches the x-axis. See the red line below, anything on this line or below this line is the feasible region.

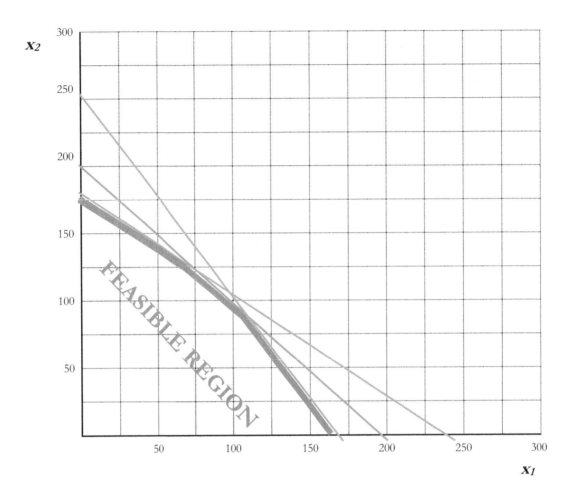

The next step to solving this graphically is to graph the profit function. The profit function we get from the objective is $\pi = 350x_1 + 300x_2$, where π is the symbol for profits. We re-write the profit function with x_2 as the y variable so we can graph it out, and you get the following:

$$x_2 = \frac{\pi}{300} - \frac{350}{300}x_1$$

This is hard to graph, because you don't know profits. The thought process is that you choose a level of profits, graph it out and see if any points along the profit line are feasible.

Let's see if \$30,000 in profits is feasible. The new profit function would then by

$$x_2 = \frac{30,000}{300} - \frac{350}{300}x_1 = 100 - \frac{7}{6}x_1$$

We can graph that out is the following way (see the black line for the profit function):

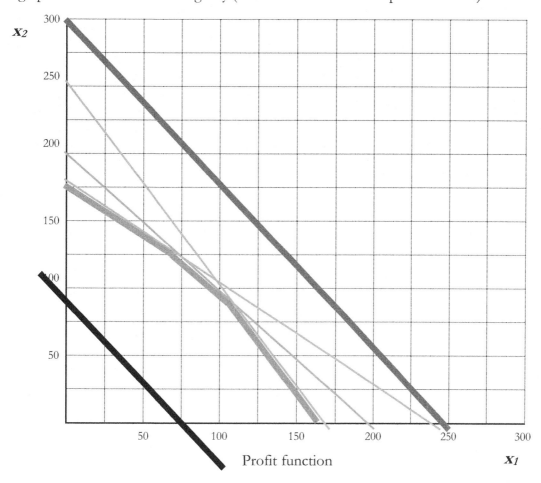

Profit function

There are many combinations of x_1 and x_2 that can produce \$30,000 in profits, all of which are feasible (since they are in the feasible region) as the black line in the graph above shows.

If we can make \$30,000 in profits, why can we not make \$90,000? Let's see if that is possible. The equation we want to graph is:

$$x_2 = \frac{90,000}{300} - \frac{350}{300}x_1 = 300 - \frac{7}{6}x_1$$

This function is shown by the purple line in the graph above. Notice that not a single point on this potential profit function is in the feasible region. Therefore, it is just not feasible, with the current constraints to make \$90,000 in profits.

Rather than jump from \$30,000 to 90,000, you can increase profits by smaller increments, this will cause the black line to shift up. You keep doing this until you reach the most extreme point where profits are the highest and there is a set of x_1, x_2 that is still in the feasible region.

In these examples, we can use the Extreme Point Theorem. This Theorem says that a solution to the linear program will be a corner point (the x and y-intercepts) or an interior kink (where two constraints intersect). We call these corner solutions.

So in this example, the four corner solutions are
1. Where the green line meets the y-axis
2. Where the blue and green line intersect
3. Where the blue and orange line intersect
4. Where the orange line meets the x-axis

Note: corner solutions satisfy all three constraints

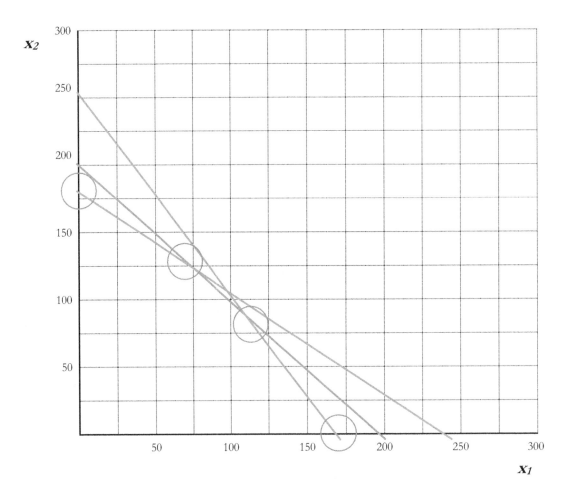

To find the x_1, x_2 values of each corner solution, we look to see where the lines intersect and then use the profit function to calculate the total profits at each point.
1. Where the green line meets the y-axis

$$x_2 = 180 - \frac{3}{4}(0) = 180 \qquad\qquad (0,180)$$
$$\pi = 350(0) + 300(180) = 54,000$$

2. Where the blue and green line intersect

$$200 - x_1 = 180 - \frac{3}{4}x_1$$ (80,120)

$$\pi = 350(80) + 300(120) = 64{,}000$$

3. Where the blue and orange line intersect

$$200 - x_1 = 261 - \frac{3}{2}x_1$$ (122,78)

$$\pi = 350(122) + 300(78) = 66{,}100$$

4. Where the orange line meets the x-axis

$$0 = 261 - \frac{3}{2}x_1$$ (174,0)

$$\pi = 350(174) + 300(0) = 60{,}900$$

From this we see that the solution is to produce 122 AS spas and 78 HLS spas. This will use all of the pumps and labor (those are the binding constraints) and we will have leftover feet of tubing. Doing so will provide the company with $66,100 in profits.

One way we can check out answer is to look at the slopes of the profit function and constraints. Again the profit function is $x_2 = 300 - \frac{7}{6}x_1$. This is a slope of -1.16.

We can look at the slopes of the constraints:

Constraint	Equation	Slope
Pumps	$x_2 \leq 200 - x_1$	-1
Labor	$x_2 \leq 261 - \frac{3}{2}x_1$	-1.5
Tubing	$x_2 \leq 180 - \frac{3}{4}x_1$	-.75

The slope of the profit function falls in between the slopes of the pumps and labor (-1.16 is between -1 and -1.5). This tells us that these will be the two binding constraint.

If the slope of the profit function was -0.9, then the pumps and tubing would be the binding constraints. If the slope of the profit function was -2, then labor would be the only binding constraint, meaning that the optimal solution would where the labor curve crosses the x-axis.

See the Videos:
https://www.youtube.com/watch?v=DxXiGSDtabI
https://www.youtube.com/watch?v=nAHnk3hKW7o
https://www.youtube.com/watch?v=XLXYNaD--3g
https://www.youtube.com/watch?v=7xxKQtmEwqA

Graphing it out in Excel

https://youtu.be/ua9gnJY4nRY

Example 4.1a. Graphing the constraints and identifying the feasible region

Maximize profits
Such that
$(i)\ x_1 + x_2 \leq 150$
$(ii)\ 2x_1 + 3x_2 \leq 420$
$(iii)\ 3x_1 + 2x_2 \leq 420$

a)   Graph all three constraints.
b)   Identify the feasible region
c)   Identify the corner solutions (extreme point theorem)
d)   Solve for the possible solutions
e)   What does the profit function tell us about the optimal solution?

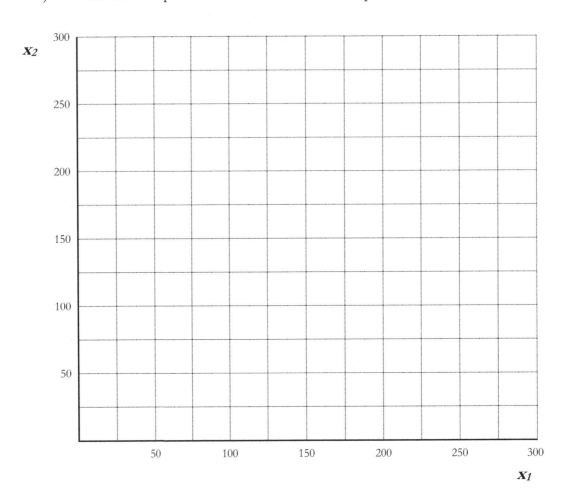

Solution Example 4.1a

First, rewrite the constraints solving for x_2

(i) $x_2 \leq 150 - x_1$

(ii) $x_2 \leq 140 - \frac{2}{3}x_1$

(iii) $x_2 \leq 210 - \frac{3}{2}x_1$

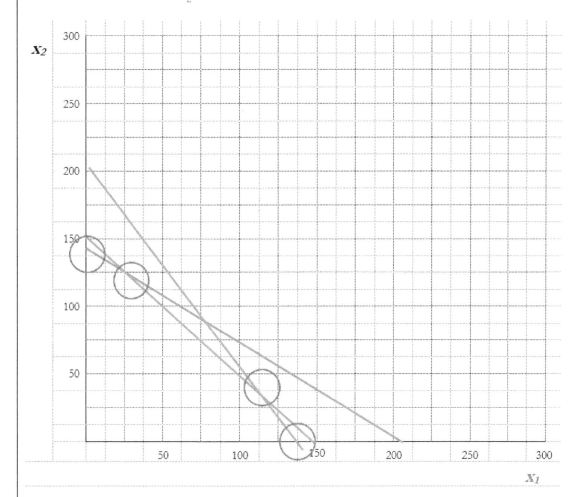

4 Optimal Solutions: (0,140), (30,120), (120,30), (140,0)

The ratio of the change in profit from producing one more good of x_2 compared to producing one more unit of x_1 will inform what the optimal solution is. If that ratio is < 2/3 then the optimal solution is (0,140). If the ratio is between 2/3 and 1, then the optimal solution is (30,120). If the ratio is between 1 and 3/2 then the optimal solution is (120, 30). If the optimal solution is greater than 3/2, the optimal solution is (140,0). Notice that those numbers comes from the slopes when graphing the constraints.

See the Video: https://www.youtube.com/watch?v=hqnjlLkJdA4

137

Example 4.1b   Agrow, Inc. mixes fertilizer from two basic inputs. One unit of fertilizer is supposed to provide a minimum of 45 units of phosphates, 48 units of potash and 84 units of nitrates. One input provides 3 units of phosphates, 4 units of potash and 14 units of nitrates. A second input provides 9 units of phosphates, 6 units of potash and 7 units of nitrates. The cost of the first input is $12 per unit; the cost of the second is $20 per unit. Find the least-cost way to mix a batch.

Write out the Linear Program:

Graph out the Feasible Region and the optimal solution

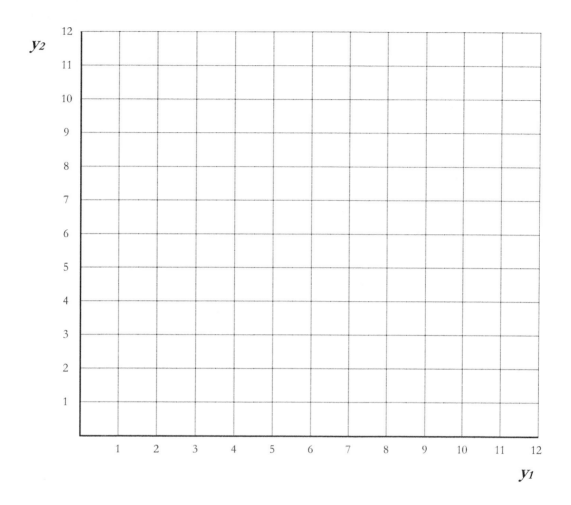

Solution Example 4.1b

Write out the linear Program:

Let y_1 = amount of input 1 to use in batch
y_2 = amount of input 2 to use in batch

Min $cost = 12y_1 + 20y_2$

s.t. $3y_1 + 9y_2 \geq 45$ Phosphates
$4y_1 + 6y_2 \geq 48$ Potash
$14y_1 + 7y_2 \geq 84$ Nitrates

To graph it out, start with the constraints and re-write them as $y = mx + b$

$y_2 \geq \dfrac{45}{9} - \dfrac{3}{9}y_1$ Phosphates   (blue line)

$y_2 \geq \dfrac{48}{6} - \dfrac{4}{6}y_1$ Potash   (orange line)

$y_2 \geq \dfrac{84}{7} - \dfrac{14}{7}y_1$ Nitrates   (green line)

Graph these out (see graph on next page)
Four possible solutions:
     1. y-intercept   (0,12)
     2. Where orange and green cross
         $\dfrac{48}{6} - \dfrac{4}{6}y_1 = \dfrac{84}{7} - \dfrac{14}{7}y_1$ (3,6)
     3. Where the orange and blue cross
         $\dfrac{48}{6} - \dfrac{4}{6}y_1 = \dfrac{45}{9} - \dfrac{3}{9}y_1$ (9,2)
     4. x-intercept   (15,0)

We can then look at the cost function for each of those four points
     1. $12(0) + 20(12) = 240$
     2. $12(3) + 20(6) = 156$
     3. $12(9) + 20(2) = 148$
     4. $12(15) + 20(0) = 180$

So the optimal solution is the third point, or (9,2)

Graph out the constraints and identify the feasible region then solve for the optimal solution

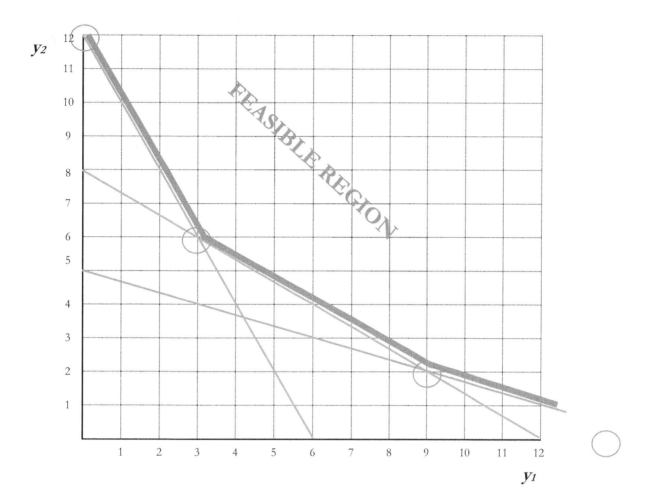

See the Video: https://www.youtube.com/watch?v=DSjJCCdUCC0

Chapter 4.2 Solving Linear Programming with Solver

Solving linear programs graphically is a good process to understand how linear programs are solved. However, as problems become more complex, solving a linear program graphically is just not practical or even possible. This is where we will turn to Solver to solve a linear program.

Solver has three parts:
        Set Objective
        By Changing Variable Cells
        Subject to the Constraints

These are the same three parts to a linear program
        Define the variable
        Identify the objective function
        Write out each constraint

Let's go back to the Example 4.1b, this is the example of Agrow mixing fertilizer from two inputs. The linear program can be written out in the following way:

Let y_1 = amount of input 1 to use in batch
      y_2 = amount of input 2 to use in batch

Min $cost = 12y_1 + 20y_2$

s.t. $3y_1 + 9y_2 \geq 45$ Phosphates
      $4y_1 + 6y_2 \geq 48$ Potash
      $14y_1 + 7y_2 \geq 84$ Nitrates

Open up Solver and you can see where each part goes.

The objective goes here

The cells representing the variables goes here

Then the constraints go here, there are three different constraints. You click Add to add each constraint.

The click solve. Boom Baby!! Problem solved.

Video Using Solver: https://www.youtube.com/watch?v=oAIplqdCIcU

Chapter 4.3 Sensitivity Analysis and Shadow Prices

Back in chapter 3, when we were doing constrained optimization problems, we ran a sensitivity report in Solver to get the Lagrange multiplier. We interpreted the Lagrange multiplier (λ) as the change in the objective function for a change in the constraint. We can do the same thing with linear program examples.

After setting up the Linear Program in Solver there are different methods that Excel uses to solve the linear program:

☑ Ma<u>k</u>e Unconstrained Variables Non-Negative

S<u>e</u>lect a Solving
Method: | GRG Nonlinear ▾ | | O<u>p</u>tions |

Solving Method

Select the GRG Nonlinear engine for Solver Problems that are smooth nonlinear. Select the LP Simplex engine for linear Solver Problems, and select the Evolutionary engine for Solver problems that are non-smooth.

| <u>H</u>elp | | <u>S</u>olve | | Cl<u>o</u>se |

GRG Nonlinear is the default option. Choosing different options will not change your final answer, but it will change the format of the reports provided. In this course we focus primarily on the Sensitivity Report. The GRN Nonlinear method will produce a report with the Lagrange Multipliers.

The other method, Simplex LP, is the method recommended for solving linear programs. Again, it will give you the same answer, but the sensitivity report is more detailed. This report gives the value of a Lagrange Multiplier but it calls it by a different name, shadow price.

The shadow price is the same thing as the Lagrange Multiplier and it comes with the same interpretation. The shadow price is the change in the objective function for a change in the constraint.

In addition to the shadow price, the report provides bounds under which the shadow price is constant. For example, if the shadow price is 2, then a 1 unit increase in the constraint will lead to a 2 unit change in the objective function. Similarly, if you increase the constraint by 10 units, you might surmise that the objective function will increase by 20 units. This may not be true. As long as the change in the objective function is within the allowable increase and the allowable decrease, the shadow price is constant and you can simply multiply it by the change.

Continuing the example above, suppose the shadow price is 2 and the allowable increase is 5 and the allowable decrease is 15. Then if the question asked, how does the objective function change when the constraint is increased by 10? You cannot answer that question with the shadow price since the increase of 10 is outside of the allowable increase (to solve this you would change the constraint and then re-run Solver). However, if the question asked, how does the objective function change when the constraint is decreased by 10? Since the allowable decrease is 15, then we can multiply the change by the shadow price and say that the objective function would decrease by 20 with a decrease of 10 in the constraint.

We say that shadow prices are constant within a specific range and running a sensitivity report using Simplex LP will provide the range under which each shadow price is constant.

Example 4.3a Using Example 4.1b, solve the linear program using Simplex LP, calculate the shadow prices, and interpret each one.

Estimating the linear program and then running a sensitivity report using Simplex LP provides the following report:

Constraints

Cell	Name	Final Value	Shadow Price	Constraint R.H. Side	Allowable Increase	Allowable Decrease
$D$7	Phosphates Amount Used	45	0.444444444	45	18	9
$D$8	Potash Amount Used	48	2.666666667	48	12	9.6
$D$9	Nitrates Amount Used	140	0	84	56	1E+30

The shadow price is interpreted as the change in the objective function for a change in the constraint. In this example the objective function is total cost.

An increase in the requirement of units of phosphates by one, increases costs by $0.44. This increase will be constant for an increase of 18 units. Increasing the constraint by 18 units, or going from a required 45 unites to 63 units, increases the costs by $18 \times 0.44 = \$7.92$. Any increase above that, requires that you re-estimate the linear program.

An increase in the requirement of units of potash by one, increases costs by $2.67. Conversely, if the required amount were to decrease from 40 to 48 (a decrease of 8 which is within the allowable decrease), then costs would decrease by $8 \times 2.67 = \$21.36$.

Increase the amount of nitrates required will have no impact on the costs (shadow price of 0) as long as the increase is 56 units or less.

Linear Program Example 1

A furniture manufacturer produces two types of tables (country and contemporary) using three types of machines. The time required to product the tables on each machine is given in the following table.

Machine	Country	Contemporary	Total Machine Time Available per Week
Router	1.5	2.0	1,000
Sander	3.0	4.5	2,000
Polisher	2.5	1.5	1,500

Country tables sell for $350 and contemporary tables sell for $450. Management has determined that at least 20% of the tables made should be country and at least 30% should be contemporary. How many of each type of table should the company produce if it wants to maximize its revenue?

Write out the Linear Program and then solve. Interpret the shadow prices.

Step 1: Define the variables:

Let x_1 be the number of country tables made

Let x_2 be the number of contemporary tables made

Step 2:   Define the objective function:
$$Max\ revenue = 350x_1 + 450x_2$$

Step 3: Define the constraints:

$(i)\ 1.5x_1 + 2x_2 \leq 1,000$ (Router Constraint)

$(ii)\ 3x_1 + 4.5x_2 \leq 2,000$ (Sander Constraint)

$(iii)\ 2.5x_1 + 1.5x_2 \leq 1,500$ (Polisher Constraint)

$(iv)\ x_1 \geq (.20)(x_1 + x_2)$ (20% Country Table Constraint)

$(v)\ x_2 \geq (.30)(x_1 + x_2)$ (30% Contemporary Table Constraint)

See video: https://www.youtube.com/watch?v=5Fzdw1Ub9pE

Solving in Excel

	Country	Contemporary		
Number of	406	174		
			Total Revenue	
Revenue	350	450	220290	
			Time Used	Time Available
Router	1.5	2	957	1,000
Sander	3	4.5	2000	2,000
Polisher	2.5	1.5	1275	1,500
Management				
Percent Required	20%	30%		
Number Required	116	174		

Note: Double click on image above to open in Excel and see formulas used

Router, Polisher, and Country requirement all have a shadow price of 0, meaning that increases in the constraints will have no change in revenues (under a certain range).

Shadow price sander = 110.14. Increasing the hours available for sanding will increase revenues by $110.14.

Shadow price contemporary = -65.22. Increasing the number of contemporary tables that management requires decreases revenues by $65.22.

See YouTube channel for solution https://www.youtube.com/watch?v=hd2mIUhio-U

Linear Program Example 2

A company is trying to determine how to allocate its $145,000 advertising budget for a new product. The company is considering newspaper ads and television commercials as its primary means for advertising. The following table summarizes the costs of advertising in these different media and the number of new customers reached by increasing amounts of advertising.

Media & # of Ads	Customers Reached	# of New Cost per Ad
Newspaper: 1-10	900	$1,000
Newspaper: 11-20	700	$900
Newspaper: 21-30	400	$800
Television: 1-5	10,000	$12,000
Television: 6-10	7,500	$10,000
Television: 11-15	5,000	$8,000

For instance, each of the first ten ads the company places in newspapers will cost $1,000 and is expected to reach 900 new customers. Each of the next 10 newspaper ads will cost $900 and is expected to reach 700 new customers. Note that the number of new customers reached by increasing amounts of advertising decreases as the advertising saturates the market. Assume the company will purchase no more than 30 newspaper ads and no more than 15 television ads. Formulate an LP model for this problem to maximize the number of new customers reached by advertising.

Solution LP Example 2

Step 1: Define the variables

Let x_1 = Number of Newspaper Ads 1-10

x_2 = Number of Newspaper Ads 11-20

x_3 = Number of Newspaper Ads 21-30

x_4 = Number of TV Ads 1-5

x_5 = Number of TV Ads 6-10

x_6 = Number of TV Ads 11-15

Step 2: Define the Objective

Max New Customers = $900x_1 + 700x_2 + 400x_3 + 10,000x_4 + 7,500x_5 + 5,000x_6$

Step 3: Define the Constraints

Budget: $1000x_1 + 900x_2 + 800x_3 + 12,000x_4 + 10,000x_5 + 8,000x_6 \leq 145,000$

Total newspaper ads $\qquad x_1 + x_2 + x_3 \leq 30$

Total tv ads $\qquad x_4 + x_5 + x_6 \leq 15$

Individual newspaper ads $\qquad x_1, x_2, x_3 \leq 10$

Individual tv ads $\qquad x_4, x_5, x_6 \leq 5$

Excel set up

Media & # of Ads	# of Ads	Customers Reached	Cost per Ad	Upper Limit
Newspaper: 1-10	10	900	$1,000	10
Newspaper: 11-20	10	700	$900	10
Newspaper: 21-30	0	400	$800	10
Television: 1-5	5	10,000	$12,000	5
Television: 6-10	5	7,500	$10,000	5
Television: 11-15	2	5,000	$8,000	5
		New Customers	145000	
		113500	145,000	
Total Newspaper	20	30		
Total Tv	12	15		

See Video for Linear Program Set Up: https://www.youtube.com/watch?v=qkDpZZqgVvY

See YouTube channel for solution https://www.youtube.com/watch?v=XQNWNJIQ0Vg

Linear Program Example 3

Max Products (MP) is the world's leading manufacturer of slip rings. A slip ring is an electrical coupling device that allows current to pass through a spinning or rotating connection—such as a gun turret on a ship, aircraft, or tank. The company recently received a $750,000 order for various quantities of three types of slip rings. Each slip ring requires a certain amount of time to wire and harness. The following table summarizes the requirements for the three models of slip rings:

	Model 1	Model 2	Model 3
Number Ordered	3,000	2,000	900
Hours of Wiring Required per Unit	2	1.5	3
Hours of Harnessing Required per Unit	1	2	1

Unfortunately, MP does not have enough wiring and harnessing capacity to fill the order by its due date. The company has only 10,000 hours of wiring capacity and 5,000 hours of harnessing capacity available to devote to this order. However, the company can subcontract any portion of this order to one of its competitors. The unit cost of producing each model in-house and buying the finished products from a competitor are summarized below.

	Model 1	Model 2	Model 3
Cost to Make	$50	$83	$130
Cost to Buy	$61	$97	$145

MP wants to determine the number of slip rings to make and the number to buy to fill the customer order at the least possible cost.

Solution Linear Program Example 3

Step 1: Define Variables

Let
$$x_1 = \textit{Number of M1 to make}$$
$$x_2 = \textit{Number of M2 to make}$$
$$x_3 = \textit{Number of M3 to make}$$
$$x_4 = \textit{Number of M1 to buy}$$
$$x_5 = \textit{Number of M2 to buy}$$
$$x_6 = \textit{Number of M3 to buy}$$

Step 2: Define Objective

$$\text{Min costs} = 50x_1 + 83x_2 + 130x_3 + 61x_4 + 97x_5 + 145x_6$$

Step 3: Define the constraints

$x_1 + x_4 \geq 3000$	Need to fill the order of 3000 M1
$x_2 + x_5 \geq 2000$	Need to fill the order of 2000 M2
$x_3 + x_6 \geq 900$	Need to fill the order of 900 M3
$2x_1 + 1.5x_2 + 3x_3 \leq 10,000$	Wiring
$1x_1 + 2x_2 + 1x_3 \leq 5,000$	Harnessing

Excel Set Up

Number to	Model 1	Model 2	Model 3		
Make	3,000	550	900		
Buy	0	1450	0		
Cost to					
Make	50	83	130	Total Costs	
Buy	61	97	145	453300	

	Model 1	Model 2	Model 3	Hours Used	Hours Available
Hours of Wiring Required per Unit	2	1.5	3	9525	10,000
Hours of Harnessing Required per Unit	1	2	1	5000	5,000
Amount Produced	3,000	2,000	900		
Order Number	3000	2000	900		

See Video for Linear Program Set Up   https://www.youtube.com/watch?v=McKnAie9Cjk
See YouTube channel for solution   https://www.youtube.com/watch?v=FzHV9AGmlMM

Linear Program Example 4

A financial analyst has just completed a consultation with a client who expects to have $750,000 in liquid assets to invest when she retires next month. The analyst and his client agreed to consider upcoming bond issues from the following six companies:

Company	Return	Years to Maturity	Rating
Acme Chemical	8.65%	11	1-Excellent
DynaStar	9.50%	10	3-Good
Eagle Vision	10.00%	6	4-Fair
MicroModeling	8.75%	10	1-Excellent
OptiPro	9.25%	7	3-Good
Sabre Systems	9.00%	13	2-Very Good

The column labeled "Return" represents the expected annual yield on each bond, the column labeled "Years to Maturity" indicates the length of time over which the bonds will be payable, and the column labeled "Rating" indicates an independent underwriter's assessment of the quality or risk associated with each issue.

The analyst believes that all of the companies are relatively safe investments. However, to protect his client's income, the analyst thinks that no more than 25% of the money should be invested in any one investment and at least half of the money should be invested in long-term bonds that mature in ten or more years. Also, even though DynaStar, Eagle Vision, and OptiPro offer the highest returns, it was agreed that no more then 35% of the money should be invested in these bonds because they also represent the highest risks (i.e., they were rated lower than "very good).

The analyst wants to determine how to allocate his client's investments to maximize her income while meeting their agreed upon investment restrictions.

Solution Linear Program Example 4

Step 1: Define the variables

Let x_1 = dollars invested in AC

x_2 = dollars invested in DS

x_3 = dollars invested in EV

x_4 = dollars invested in MM

x_5 = dollars invested in OP

x_6 = dollars invested in SS

Step 2: Define the objective

Max return = $0.0865x_1 + 0.095x_2 + 0.1x_3 + 0.0875x_4 + 0.0925x_5 + 0.09x_6$

Step 3: Define the constraints

$$x_1 + x_2 + x_3 + x_4 + x_5 + x_6 = 750{,}000$$
$$x_i \leq (750{,}000)(0.25) \qquad \text{for each } i = 1, \dots, 6$$
$$x_1 + x_2 + x_4 + x_6 \geq (750{,}000)(0.5)$$
$$x_2 + x_3 + x_5 \leq (750{,}000)(0.35)$$

Excel Set Up:

Company	Amount invested in	Return	amount invested	Individual Max 25%	Years to Maturity	10+ years	Rating	Good or Fair
Acme Chemical	112500	8.65%	$ 112,500	$ 187,500	11	1	1-Excellent	0
DynaStar	75000	9.50%	$ 75,000	$ 187,500	10	1	3-Good	1
Eagle Vision	187500	10.00%	$ 187,500	$ 187,500	6	0	4-Fair	1
MicroModeling	187500	8.75%	$ 187,500	$ 187,500	10	1	1-Excellent	0
OptiPro	0	9.25%	$ -	$ 187,500	7	0	3-Good	1
Sabre Systems	187500	9.00%	$ 187,500	$ 187,500	13	1	2-Very Good	0
		Total Return				562500		262500
Total Invested	750000	68887.5		Max		375000		262500
Total to Invest	750,000			25%				

Note: Double click on the image above to open in Excel

See Video for Linear Program Set Up   https://www.youtube.com/watch?v=8nBB_9Bv_1Q

See YouTube channel for solution   https://www.youtube.com/watch?v=Gg5XckqRsWY

Linear Program Example 5

Tempsun is a leading grower and distributor of fresh peaches with three large peach groves scattered around central Florida in the cities of Mt. Dora, Eustis, and Clermont. Tempsun currently has 275,000 bushels of peaches at the grove in Mt. Dora, 400,000 bushels at the grove in Eustis, and 300,000 bushels at the grove in Clermont. Tempsun has peach processing plants in Ocala, Orlando, and Leesburg with processing capacities to handle 200,000, 600,000, and 225,000 bushels, respectively. Tempsun contracts with a local trucking company to transport its fruit from the groves to the processing plants. The trucking company charges a flat rate for every mile that each bushel of fruit must be transported. Each mile a bushel of fruit travels is known as a bushel-mile. The following table summarizes the distances (in miles) between the groves and processing plants:

Distances (in miles) Between Groves and Plants

Grove	Ocala	Orlando	Leesburg
Mt. Dora	21	50	40
Eustis	35	30	22
Clermont	55	20	25

Tempsun wants to determine how many bushels to ship from each grove to each processing plant to minimize the total number of bushel-miles the fruit must be shipped.

Solution Linear Program Example 5

Step 1: Define Variables
Let

x_1 = number of bushels shipped from Mt Dora to Ocala
x_2 = number of bushels shipped from Mt Dora to Orlando
x_3 = number of bushels shipped from Mt Dora to Leesburg
x_4 = number of bushels shipped from Eustis to Ocala
x_5 = number of bushels shipped from Eustis to Orlando
x_6 = number of bushels shipped from Eustis to Leesburg
x_7 = number of bushels shipped from Clermont to Ocala
x_8 = number of bushels shipped from Clermont to Orlando
x_9 = number of bushels shipped from Clermont to Leesburg

Step 2: Define Objective
Min bushel miles = $21x_1 + 50x_2 + 40x_3 + 35x_4 + 30x_5 + 22x_6 + 55x_7 + 20x_8 + 25x_9$

Step 3: Define Constraints
$x_1 + x_2 + x_3 = 275{,}000$
$x_4 + x_5 + x_6 = 400{,}000$
$x_7 + x_8 + x_9 = 300{,}000$
$x_1 + x_4 + x_7 \leq 200{,}000$
$x_2 + x_5 + x_8 \leq 600{,}000$
$x_3 + x_6 + x_9 \leq 225{,}000$

Set up in Excel

Distances (in miles)
Between Groves and Plants

Grove	Ocala	Orlando	Leesburg	Supply
Mt. Dora	21	50	40	275,000
Eustis	35	30	22	400,000
Clermont	55	20	25	300,000
Capacity	200,000	600,000	225,000	

Between Groves and Plants

Grove	Ocala	Orlando	Leesburg	
Mt. Dora	200000	0	75000	275000
Eustis	0	250000	150000	400000
Clermont	0	300000	0	300000
bushels received	200000	550000	225000	
		Total Distance (bushel miles)	24000000	

See Video for Set Up https://www.youtube.com/watch?v=NMn7bkWRADc
See Video for Solver https://www.youtube.com/watch?v=EkazIjoZk1k

Linear Program Example 6

MorningStar is a company that sells agricultural products to farmers in several states. One service it provides to customers is custom feed mixing, whereby a farmer can order a specific amount of livestock feed and specify the amount of corn, grain, and minerals the feed should contain. This is an important service because the proper feed for various farm animals changes regularly depending on the weather, pasture conditions, and so on.

MorningStar stocks bulk amounts of four types of feeds that it can mix to meet a given customer's specifications. The following table summarizes the four feeds, their composition of corn, grain, and minerals, and the cost per pound for each type.

	Percent of Nutrition in			
	Feed 1	Feed 2	Feed 3	Feed 4
Corn	30%	5%	20%	10%
Grains	10%	30%	15%	10%
Minerals	20%	20%	20%	30%
Cost per Pound	$0.25	$0.30	$0.32	$0.15

On average, U.S. citizens consume almost 70 pounds of poultry per year. To remain competitive, chicken growers must ensure that they feed the required nutrients to their flocks in the most cost-effective manner. MorningStar has just received an order from a local chicken farmer for 8,000 pound of feed. The farmer wants this feed to contain at least 20% corn, 15% grain, and 15% minerals. What should MorningStar do to fill this order at minimum cost?

Step1: Define the variables

Let

$$x_1 = \text{pounds of feed 1}$$
$$x_2 = \text{pounds of feed 2}$$
$$x_3 = \text{pounds of feed 3}$$
$$x_4 = \text{pounds of feed 4}$$

Step 2: Define the objective

$$\text{Min costs} = .25x_1 + .30x_2 + .32x_3 + .15x_4$$

Step 3: Define the constraints

$$x_1 + x_2 + x_3 + x_4 = 8,000$$
$$.3x_1 + .05x_2 + .2x_3 + .1x_4 \geq (8,000)(.20)$$
$$.1x_1 + .3x_2 + .15x_3 + .1x_4 \geq (8,000)(.15)$$
$$.20x_1 + .2x_2 + .2x_3 + .3x_4 \geq (8,000)(.20)$$

Set up in Excel

	Percent of Nutrition in						
	Feed 1	Feed 2	Feed 3	Feed 4	Used	Required	
Corn	30%	5%	20%	10%	1600	1600	20%
Grains	10%	30%	15%	10%	1200	1200	15%
Minerals	20%	20%	20%	30%	1750	1600	20%
Cost per Pound	$0.25	$0.30	$0.32	$0.15			

	Feed 1	Feed 2	Feed 3	Feed 4		Total Cost	
Pounds of	4500	2000	0	1500		1950	

	Used	Required
8,000 lbs	8000	8,000

See Video for Linear Program Set Up   https://www.youtube.com/watch?v=pebcMgRBo48

See YouTube channel for solution   https://www.youtube.com/watch?v=zbFTAfSwoQc

Linear Programming Example 7

The marketing manager for Power by Price needs to decide how many TV spots and magazine ads to run during the next quarter. Each TV spot costs $5,000 and is expected to increase sales by 300,000 units. Each magazine ad costs $2,000 and is expected to increase sales by 500,000 units. A total of $100,000 will be spent on TV and magazine ads; however, Power by Price wants to spend no more than $70,000 on TV spots and no more than $50,000 on magazine ads. Power by Price is maximizing revenue and receives $1 for each unit it sells.

1. Formulate an LP model for this problem
2. Solve the problem using Solver
3. Using the sensitivity report, provide a consultation for my business.

Step 1: Defined the variables

Let x_1 = number of TV ads

x_2 = number of magazine ads

Step 2: Define the objective

Objective Max sales = $300,000x_1 + 500,000x_2$

Step 3: Define Constraints

$(i) 5,000x_1 + 2,000x_2 \leq 100,000$

$(ii) 5,000x_1 \leq 70,000$

$(iii) 2,000x_2 \leq 50,000$

Set up in Excel

	x1	x2		
	10	25	Sales	
sales per ad	300000	500000	15500000	
			Paid	Budget
cost	5000	2000	100000	100000
Amount Spent	50,000	50,000		
Spend no more than	70000	50000		

Sensitivity Report

Cell	Name		Final Value	Shadow Price	Constraint R.H. Side	Allowable Increase	Allowable Decrease
$B$7	Amount Spent	x1	50000	0	70000	1E+30	20000
$C$7	Amount Spent	x2	50000	190	50000	50000	20000
$D$5	cost	Paid	100000	60	100000	20000	50000

Increasing the budget of $100,000 by $1 will lead to 60 more sales. This $1 increase is constant until the budget is increased by more than $20,000.

Constraint of spending no more than $50,000 on Magazine ads is binding, and if you can convince management to relax this contrainst, each additional dollar spent on magazine ads will increase sales by 190. It will be 190 as long as you spend no more than $100,000 (original $50,000 + allowable increase of $50,000). After that, it is different than $60.

Linear Programming Example 8
(Think you got the hang of Linear Programming? Give this monster a shot)

Snow Bunny operates a clothing store specializing in ski apparel. Given the seasonal nature of its business, often there is an imbalance between when bills must be paid for inventory purchased and when the goods actually are sold and cash is received. Over the next six months, the company expects cash receipts and requirements for bill paying as follows:

	Month					
	1	2	3	4	5	6
Cash Receipts	100,000	$225,000	$275,000	$350,000	$475,000	$625,000
Bills Due	$400,000	$500,000	$600,000	$300,000	$200,000	$100,000

The company likes to maintain a cash balance of at least $20,000 and currently has $100,000 cash on hand. The company can borrow money from a local bank for the following term / rate structure: 1 month at 1%, 2 months at 1.75%, 3 months at 2.49%, 4 months at 3.22% and 5 months at 3.94%. When needed, money is borrowed at the end of a month and repaid, with interest, at the end of the month in which the obligation is due. For instance, if the company borrows $10,000 for 2 months in month 3, it would have to pay back $10,175 at the end of month 5. Determine the borrowing and cash flow plan that minimizes financing costs while meeting cash needs.

For Solutions: watch videos
See Video for Linear Program Set Up   https://www.youtube.com/watch?v=a21orWOyxgo
See YouTube channel for solution   https://www.youtube.com/watch?v=VP1GUwrqyb8

Chapter 5
Data Analysis

Back in 2000, there was a serial killer called The Citizen who threatened that his next victim would be the winner of Miss United States Beauty Pageant. Gracie Hart, a phenomenal FBI agent went undercover to be ever-present during the pageant and provide the FBI with information about who The Citizen might be. In the course of the investigation, Agent Hart learned that this threat was not from The Citizen, but a copycat criminal seeking to ruin those in charge of the pageant. Unknown to anyone, this copycat criminal actually planted a remote bomb in the tiara. When Ms. Rhode Island won Miss United States, Agent Hart was able to act quickly and prevent any loss of life. The entire investigation has been recorded in a documentary known as Miss Congeniality.

Building on that case, I present to you the following figure:

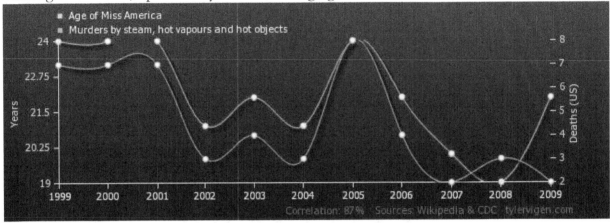

Whether you want to believe it or not, there is a relationship between the age of Miss American and the number of murders by steam, hot vapours, and hot objects. But you should be asking, what is that relationship?

The purpose of these next two sections is to understand relationships between two variables. The purpose of the Data Analysis section is to understand descriptive relationships. Can we use summary statistics (means, standard deviations) and pictures to describe relationships between two variables? The figure above might make you take a second thought about what is that relationship between the variables of age of Miss American and the number of murders by steam, hot vapours, and hot objects?

The goal is to use data to present information in a meaningful way to help answer questions you and others might have. So let's start with data.

First, data are, data is not is. That is, data is plural. I don't know why I tell you this but you might want to know. The singular form of data is datum. And now you know.

Traditional data analysis requires certain formatting for your data. The data are organized with each observation as a row, while each aspect or variable about that observation is a column. If we are measuring the height and weight of those in a classroom, each person is an observation, and each person has a weight and height.

Data that are structured for data analysis can come in many different formats:

162

Cross Sectional: data collected with multiple units of observations within a given period of time. Example: surveys done on Survey Monkey (the individual respondent is the unit of observation. Multiple people fill out the survey and do so in a given period of time.)

Time Series: data collected with a single unit of observation over a given period of time
Example: S&P 500 (the unit of observation is the value of the index and it is measured over time)

There are also hybrids of the two

Repeated Cross Section: This is a cross section data set that is collected in multiple time periods. It need not be the same individuals in each time period.
Example: US Census. Every 10 years data is collected on everyone in the United States. Individuals in the 1940 Census need not be in the 2010 Census.

Panel: data collected with multiple units of observations over a given period of time.
Example: A survey is given to all high school seniors in 1980. They are then surveyed again every two years for the next 30 years.

For this class, we will focus on Cross Sectional Data. In follow up courses: Decision Modeling (ECON 3170), Econometrics (ECON 4260), and Data Analytics (ANLY 4100) other types of data will be analyzed.

Cross Sectional data take the following format.

	Variable 1	Variable 2	Variable 3	Variable 4	Variable 5
Respondent 1					
Respondent 2					
Respondent 3					
Respondent 4					
Respondent 5					

Such that for each respondent there is a value for each variable. Often times, variables come from surveys and represent the answer a respondent gave on an individual answer on the survey.

Within excel we want to be able to analyze the data. That is we want to be able to accomplish the following:
1. Manage the data
2. Summarize the data
3. Data Visualization
4. Inference Testing

Several tools within Excel allow the user to view the data. The purpose of this section is to show you a few of these tools and learn how to use them. We will use a data set called wages.xlsx to work through this section. This data set cab be found on Canvas and the G-drive (G:/Price/data). The data comes from a paper with a fancy title, "Unobserved Ability, Efficiency Wages, and Interindustry Wage Differentials[2]." The data is a cross section of individuals responding to questions about their job in 1980.

Tool 1: Sort

In the ribbon at the top of the screen of an Excel workbook is the Data tab. In about the middle of the section is the following:

While you can use the A to Z or Z to A quick commands on the left, we are going to use the big Sort prompt. But before you click that, click on the top left box in your worksheet that is located just to the left of column A and just above row 1. This should highlight the entire worksheet. Once you have done that, then click on the Sort button.

This will bring up the following window:

The first thing to point out is in the top right, there is a box that you can click "My data has headers". If your first row is the name of the variable, or has headers, then make sure to click this box. In the data set wages.xlsx, the first row does indeed have headers so make sure you check this box.

---

[2] M. Blackburn and D. Neumark (1992), "Unobserved Ability, Efficiency Wages, and Interindustry Wage Differentials," *Quarterly Journal of Economics* 107, 1421-1436.

Let's suppose that we want to sort the data based on wages. Then where it says "Sort by", click on the variable you want to sort by, wages. The third box "Order" allows you to sort smallest to largest or you can select largest to smallest. Click OK and you have now sorted your data.

On your own: sort the data so women are first in the data set followed by men.

To do this highlight the data and go to Sort. Select "sort by" and choose the variable female. In this case you want to sort largest to smallest so that those where female=1 (indicator for respondent being a woman) are sorted first.

We can also add levels. Suppose we want to sort the data so that women come first. Then within women we want to sort them from the highest level of education listed first. We can do this by adding a level.

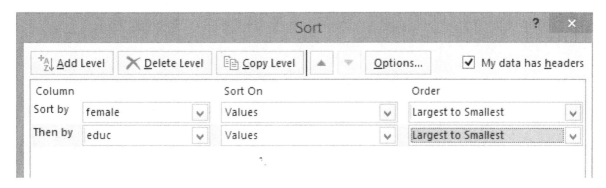

Sorting the data allows you as the user to see the data and look for patterns, oddities, or other things of interest in the data.

Tool 2: Filter
Next to Sort in the Data tab is the Filter button. Highlight the entire data set by clicking on the top left cell in the worksheet and then click the Filter button.

Doing so will create a dropdown menu for each variable. In this menu are options to sort the data, this is another useful way to sort the data. However, it does not allow you to sort with levels.

Near the bottom of the drop down menu are the actual values of that variable. To show this, click on the drop down menu for the variable female. There are three boxes with a description next to each one: Select All, 0, and 1. Notice that all three boxes are checked, this means that Excel is displaying observations that meet all the checked criteria.

To filter the data to show only those observations who are female, uncheck the box for 0, then click OK. When you do this, you will see that in the female column, it only shows values that are 1. The drop down menu changes the icon to show that this column is filtered.

Additionally, the rows on the left are now numbered in blue. This means that the data has been filtered. As you see, the rows go 1,2,3,9,10. This means that observations 4-8 were males and are not being displayed.

If you want to run an analysis on only women, then you could filter the data by female=1 and then copy and paste the data into a new worksheet. When you do, the rows on the right will be numbered in black because this new worksheet is the base data set that has not been filtered.

Suppose I want a data set that is females with 16 years of education, then I would filter for females=1 and then on education, only check the box for 16 years of education. Copy and paste that to a new worksheet and you are ready to go.

See if you can answer the following questions by using Filter.
  i.   How many respondents have no years of education?
  ii. How many married females have exactly one year of work experience?
  iii. What is the range of wages in the data set?

  See Video: https://www.youtube.com/watch?v=gwsS1BZLoV8

Top stop filtering the data, you can just click on the Filter button in the Data tab.

Tool 3: Generate new variables
There are two ways in which we can generate new variables
    (A) generate a mathematical combination of existing variables
    (B) use the if function to generate new variables

We want to create a variable for married female. That is, we want the variable to take the value of 1 when the respondent is a married female and 0 when not. That is, we want a variable, call it married female, to equal 1 if married equals 1 and female equals 1. If either of those two variables equals 0, we want married female to equal 0.

To do this, if we were to multiply the variable married by the variable female, then when both are 1, the product will be one ($1x1 = 1$). But if either or both are 0, then the product will be zero. To do this in excel, you can do the following.

In cell V2 you can insert the following code

> =F2*G2

This will create the new variable. Copy paste down to create this for all respondents.

Suppose we want to create a column for married men. This becomes more difficult because we do not have a variable that equals 1 if male. So we can create that using the IF function.

In cell W2 type the following code

> =IF(F2=0,1,0)

This command tells us that if F2=0 is true, then return the value of 1. If F2=0 is not true, then return the value of 0. The syntax for the IF function is as follows:

```
=IF(argument, return value if true, return value if false)
```

Now that there is a column for married and males, we can create a new variable which multiplies the variables married and men just like we did before.

Or we can use the IF function with and AND function to create a the same variable without having to create a new variable for males. In a new cell, use this code:

```
=IF(AND(G2=1,F2<>1),1,0)
```

What this command does is similar to the if command except we add an AND to it. For the if argument to be true, G2 must equal 1 and f2 must not equal 1. We do this with <> these two signs. If this argument is true, it will return a value of 1. If not it will return a value of 0. Note that column G is married and F is female

See Video: https://www.youtube.com/watch?v=HqM04D7s9WY

There are often many ways of answering a question in Excel. For example, we could combine some of the concepts learned above and use an N function. An N function evaluates an argument and returns a 1 if it is true and a 0 if it is false. To create a variable for both male and married we could use the following formula:

```
=N(G2=1) * N(F2<>1)
```

As you become an Excel Jedi, you will learn new ways to do things, quicker ways, better ways. This course is just to start your training. You will need to seek out your own Master Yoda to continue your training.

Lastly, we may want to convert data that is numerical to words or vice versa. The IF function can do that for us. If we want to create a variable called gender that spells out the gender of the individual, rather than give us 0 and 1's. We can do that with this formula:

```
=IF(F2=1, "female", "male")
```

This says that if cell F2=1 then return the value of "female" and if not, return the value of "male". For Excel to recognize words in a function, you need to use quotation marks.
We can reverse that, going from words to numbers, by using the variable with words to create a variable for males.

```
=IF(Z2="male",1,0)
```

These three tools: Sort, Filter, and Generate New Variables allow you as the user to manage the data. Once you have managed the data you are ready for the next section, Summarize the data.

What we want to be able to do is to come up with sample moments. You are probably familiar with the first two moments but here are the first four in case you find yourself on Jeopardy with the topic of Method of Moments.

First Moment: Mean
Second Moment: Variance
Third Moment: Skewness
Fourth Moment: Kurtosis

Sample Mean: From your statistics course (which is a prerequisite for this one) you clearly remember how to calculate the mean. But just in case you forgot, here is the equation to calculate the sample mean.

$$Sample\ Mean = \bar{x} = \frac{1}{n}\sum_{i=1}^{N} x_i$$

This is found by adding up all the values for each observation and then dividing by the number of observations. In excel this is done by using the command:

=AVERAGE(*range of observations*)

Sample Variance: tells about the spread of the data or the variation. It is calculated with the following equation:

$$Sample\ Variance = S^2 = \frac{1}{n-1}\sum_{i=1}^{N}(x_i - \bar{x})^2$$

Related to Variance is the term standard deviation. Standard deviation is just the square root of the Variance. And the sample standard deviation is known simply as S.

These two terms can be calculated in excel with the following equations:

=VAR(*range of observations*)
=STDEV(*range of observations*)

These are the older versions of the functions in Excel and even though they still work, here is the function you can use that is more up to date.

=VAR.S(*range of observations*)
=STDEV.S(*range of observations*)

With almost all of the data we will use in this class, as well as real life, you will be dealing with a sample and not the population. That is why we calculate the Variance of the Sample. The equations for population variance and sample variance are similar, but different. For a discussion on this topic check out a statistics textbook.

See the videos: https://www.youtube.com/watch?v=BK23Nfhdjt0
https://www.youtube.com/watch?v=vw_8vDNI_x4

In Excel, we can also calculate means for subsamples. For example, suppose we want to find the average years of schooling for women. We could use the Filtering tool to create a new worksheet with only females and then take the average of education. Or we can use the function AVERAGEIFS, which allows us to take the average if certain conditions are met. For this example, we could do the following:

> =AVERAGEIFS(B:B,F:F,1)

This function says take the average of column B (education) if column F (female) equals 1.

You can build on this to answer the question, what is the average years of schooling for single women. You would use the same function with an additional criteria.

> =AVERAGEIFS(B:B,F:F,1,G:G,0)

AVERAGEIFS allows you to add several criteria, if female equals 1 and if married equals 0 (meaning they are single)

Example 5.2a   **Calculate the average wage of all observations**

Example 5.2b   **Calculate the average of married. How do you interpret this?**

Example 5.2c   **What is the average wage of men?**

Example 5.2d   **What is the average wage of women?**

Example 5.2e   **What is the variance of wages?**

Example 5.2a   Calculate the average wage of all observations

=AVERAGE(A2:A527)	5.91

Example 5.2b   Calculate the average of married. How do you interpret this?

=AVERAGE(G2:G527)	0.61	61% of the sample is married

Example 5.2c   What is the average wage of men?

First you need to sort the data by female (smallest to largest). Remember when female=0 that means respondent is male

=AVERAGE(A2:A275)   7.12

or you can use the AVERAGEIFS command
=AVERAGEIFS(A:A,F:F,0)   7.12

Example 5.2d   What is the average wage of women?

If data is sorted by female,
=AVERAGE(A276:A527)   4.60

or   =AVERAGEIFS(A:A,F:F,1)   4.60

Example 5.2e   What is the variance of wages?

=VAR.S(A2:A527)

Using the IFS functions allows you to calculate important summary statistics without having to sort the data first, or without having to filter the data and then copy and paste it into a new worksheet. There are numerous functions, spend time in Excel looking at the different functions and understand what they do. Learning new functions can save you tons of time and make your analysis easier and better.

When we talk about summary statistics, we refer to statistics that can summarize the data or describe the data. Within Economics, the two most commonly reported summary statistics are mean and standard deviation. Here is an example of summary stats from an actual economic study[3]:

This summary statistics table shows the averages by subgroup, meaning that they could be created in Excel by using the AVERAGEIFS function. What this table does is allows both you and the reader to better understand the data. For example, look at the variable male. In the Standard Incentive group only 15.7 percent of that group is male, compared to 21.2 and 35.7 percent in the other groups. This shows that subjects of this study are predominantly female.

Table 4: Summary Statistics by Group

Variable	Standard Incentives			Modified Incentives			Control Group		
	Obs	Mean	Std. Dev	Obs	Mean	Std. Dev	Obs	Mean	Std. Dev
Initial BMI	1513	32.8	6.24	765	32.8	6.00	129	31.3	5.72
Male	1513	0.157	0.364	765	0.212	0.409	129	0.357	0.481
Age	1513	46.2	10.4	765	43.0	8.8	129	44.4	10.6
Height	1513	65.5	3.41	765	66.1	3.42	129	66.7	4.25
Overweight (30>BMI>=25)	1513	0.412	0.492	765	0.382	0.486	129	0.519	0.502
Obese (40>BMI>=30)	1513	0.301	0.459	765	0.314	0.464	129	0.256	0.438
Morbidly Obese (BMI>=40)	1513	0.287	0.452	765	0.305	0.461	129	0.225	0.419
Foundation exercise regimen	1513	0.601	0.490	765	0.550	0.498	129	0.488	0.502
Intermediate exercise regimen	1513	0.337	0.473	765	0.374	0.484	129	0.426	0.496
Advanced exercise regimen	1513	0.062	0.241	765	0.076	0.265	129	0.085	0.280
Email open rate	740	45.7	36.41	765	51.0	35.09	129	28.7	32.47

---

[3] Cawley, J., & Price, J. A. (2009). *Outcomes in a program that offers financial rewards for weight loss* (No. w14987). National Bureau of Economic Research.

Common functions used in Excel

If   Checks whether a condition is met, and returns one value if TRUE, and another value if FALSE.

N   If the function is true, return a 1. If the function is false, return a 0.

AND   Checks whether all arguments are TRUE, and returns TRUE if all arguments are TRUE.

OR   Checks whether any of the arguments are TRUE, and returns TRUE or FALSE. Returns FALSE only if all arguments are FALSE.

SUM   Adds all the numbers in a range of cells.

SUMIFS   Adds the cells specified by a given set of conditions or criteria.

AVERAGE   Returns the average (arithmetic mean) of its arguments, which can be numbers or names, arrays, or references that contain numbers.

AVERAGEIFS   Finds average (arithmetic mean) for the cells specified by a given set of conditions or criteria.

COUNT   Counts the number of cells in a range that contain numbers.

COUNTIFS   Counts the number of cells specified by a given set of conditions or criteria.

For more help on functions, click on the fx button just below the ribbon. This will open a Formula Builder wizard that provides more details on functions. Or you can click on the functions tab in the ribbon which categorizes the different functions.

There are many ways to present information. Graphs and figures are nice because everyone from kiddos to grandparents love pictures. There are a few rules of thumb with graphs. Lines, scatter, and bar plots are the preferred methods of visual communication. Bar plots should nearly always start at zero. Scatter is good at looking at many data points simultaneously. Lines are great to show levels, trend, and changes in direction. Except for the purpose of highlighting a single category, you should avoid using colors when possible. Although occasionally other forms of visual communication are necessary (like pie charts), line, bars, and scatter should be your go-to forms of visual communication.

Here are some examples:

Scatter Plot:

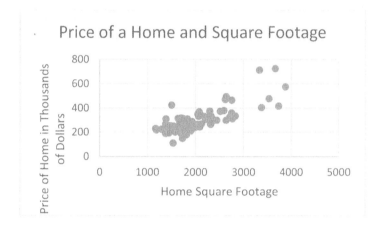

Line Plot:

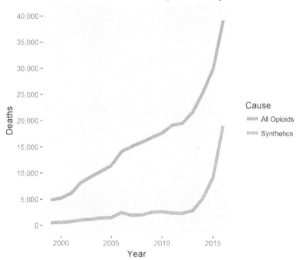

Bar chart:

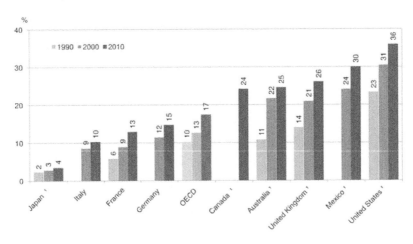

Pie Chart:

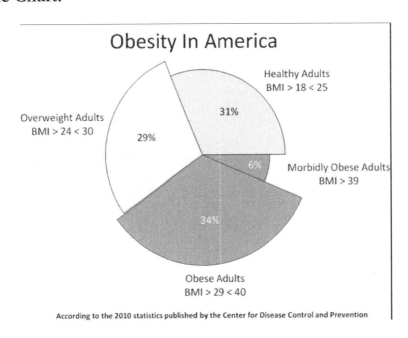

For summarizing data, the mean and standard deviation may not always accurately describe what the data look like. (This example is known as Anscombe's quartet.)

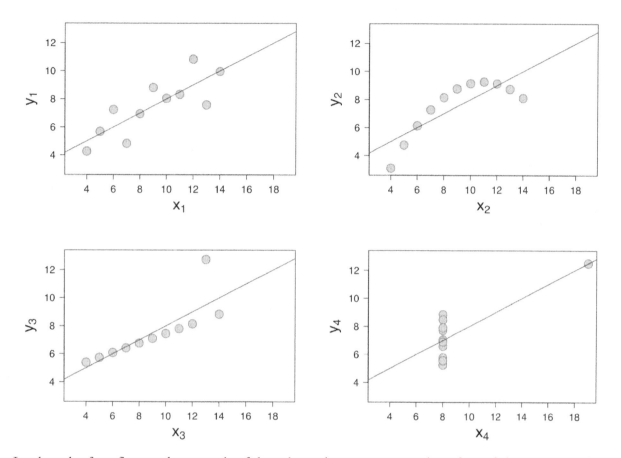

Look at the four figures above, each of them have the same mean value of x and the same standard deviation of x. A simple summary stats table of means and standard deviation will show there is no difference between the four figures.

Thus it can be very helpful to show the full distribution of the data. A histogram can do this for us.

Histogram

Like Solver, Excel has an add-on package called Data Analysis Tool Pak. If you don't see it by solver in the data tab, you will need to add it in under File> Options> Add-ins> Go.

Once we add it in, click on Data Analysis then click on histogram. A histogram is a way to show the distribution of the variable.
Once the histogram box is open:
- You will need to identify the input range, this is the data that you want to show in a histogram.
- You will need to input the bin range. If you do not enter anything here, excel will default your data into bins. Or you can create a new column and classify the bins yourself

To do this, let's look at what the distribution of wages looks like, that is create a histogram of wages.

To generate your bins, in a new column, type 0 in the first row and 1 in the second row. Highlight the two and drag it down until you get to 25. In the histogram window, highlight wages for your input and highlight the new column for your bins.

wage	bin range
3	1
6	2
5.3	3
8.8	4
11	5
18	6
8.8	7
5.5	8
22	9
17	10
8.5	11
9.6	12
7.8	13
13	14
13	15
13	16
3.5	17
14	18
1.7	19
3.7	20
5	21
6	22
2.5	23
3.3	24
10	25
4.4	

This will create a new worksheet with two columns, one with bins and one with a count of wages within that bin.

Now that you have the new worksheet, you can create a bar graph which is a histogram.

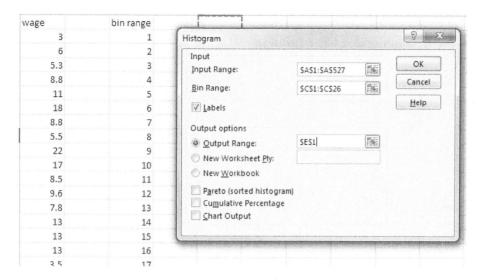

Once you click OK, it will create two new columns. One for your bin range and one for your frequency, of the number of individuals within the bin.

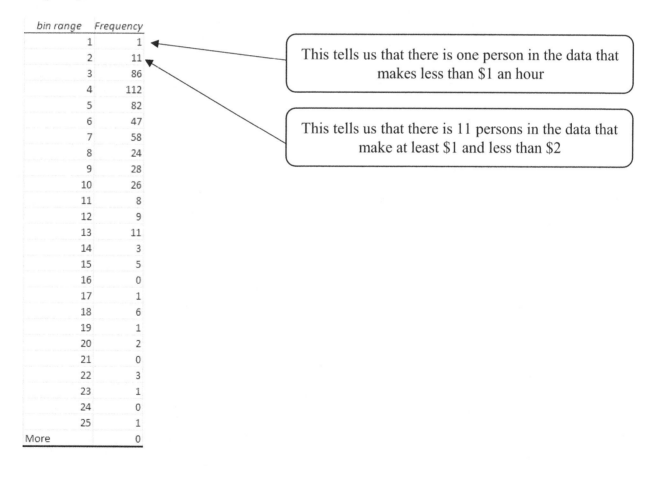

bin range	Frequency
1	1
2	11
3	86
4	112
5	82
6	47
7	58
8	24
9	28
10	26
11	8
12	9
13	11
14	3
15	5
16	0
17	1
18	6
19	1
20	2
21	0
22	3
23	1
24	0
25	1
More	0

This tells us that there is one person in the data that makes less than $1 an hour

This tells us that there is 11 persons in the data that make at least $1 and less than $2

Once we get this, we can create the actual histogram. Highlight the frequency column and go to the "Insert" tab at the top of the excel workbook.

Click on the top left icon in the Recommended Charts option:

Once you create a bar chart, make sure you have the x-axis data match that of your bin range. You may need to right click on your new chart, select data and edit your x labels

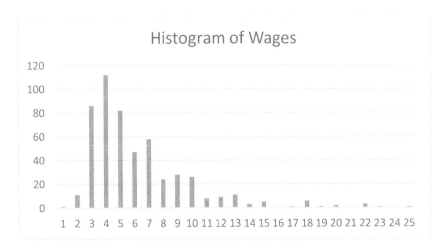

Try this with your histogram:

Instead of count as your y-axis, have it be the fraction of the sample You will need to create a new variable to graph. Instead of frequency (which is a count variable), use the fraction of the data that is in each bin.

1. Create a cell which adds up all the observations (use sum function)
2. Then create a column that divides the number of individuals in each bin by the total number in the sample.

bin range	Frequency	Percentage
1	1	=F2/$F$28
2	11	
3	86	

3. Copy and paste that all the way down
4. Use this new column to create a graph.

It should look like this:

Histogram of Wages (Percentage)

Create a histogram of wages for females and males on the same graph
    To do this you will need to sort the data by gender.
    Create bin range (here I change it just a little, I go from 2 to 13)
    Use Data Analysis > Histogram once for men and once for females
    It should look something like this:

bin range	MALES	
2	bin range	Frequency
3	2	4
4	3	25
5	4	37
6	5	42
7	6	31
8	7	32
9	8	15
10	9	22
11	10	22
12	11	6
13	12	7
	13	11
	More	19
	FEMALES	
	Bin	Frequency
	2	8
	3	60
	4	75
	5	40
	6	16
	7	26
	8	9
	9	6
	10	4
	11	2
	12	2
	13	0
	More	4

Notice that the bin range is the same for both groups. This is necessary if you are to combine them in the same histogram

Now you can use both histogram outputs to create a combined histogram. You can copy paste the females next to the males, then highlight them both and go from there. Or you can create one and then go to Select Data>add series.

If there are significant differences between the sample size of the two groups, it is advisable to create the histograms using percentages instead of frequencies.

bin range	MALES	FEMALES	MALES	FEMALES
2	4	8	0.014652	0.031746
3	25	60	0.091575	0.238095
4	37	75	0.135531	0.297619
5	42	40	0.153846	0.15873
6	31	16	0.113553	0.063492
7	32	26	0.117216	0.103175
8	15	9	0.054945	0.035714
9	22	6	0.080586	0.02381
10	22	4	0.080586	0.015873
11	6	2	0.021978	0.007937
12	7	2	0.025641	0.007937
13	11	0	0.040293	0
More	19	4	0.069597	0.015873
	273	252		

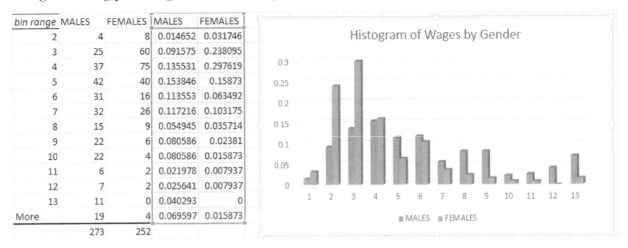

See Video: https://www.youtube.com/watch?v=9caRe02uTQ8

Chapter 5.4 Inference Testing

Inference testing is the statisticians attempt to apply the scientific method. Here we try to follow these steps:

We start with a question and construct a hypothesis that can answer the question. In statistics, we are going to form our hypothesis to equal some number. Then when we test the hypothesis using data. We just have to find one case that shows the hypothesis is wrong. If we can find one example, then we can reject the hypothesis. If we can't find an example, it does not mean that the hypothesis is guaranteed to be right, it just means that we do not have evidence to suggest that it is wrong. In these cases, we say that we fail to reject the hypothesis. This thought process is going to be incredibly important as we move forward.

Let's start with a simple example. Is the average wage of workers $6.50 per hour?

That is our question, now we construct a hypothesis. We call the null hypothesis H_o and our alternative hypothesis H_A. Our null hypothesis is that wages are $6.50. Our alternative is that they are not.

$$H_o: \beta = 6.50$$
$$H_A: \beta \neq 6.50$$

As we test this, if we can find a representative data and show just one case where in that sample the average wage is not $6.50, then we can reject the null hypothesis. If our data set is not different from $6.50, it only means that we don't have evidence to reject the null hypothesis, so we would say that we fail to reject the null hypothesis.

We are not testing if wages are less than 6.50 or greater than (that would be a one-tailed test), are testing if it is different than 6.50, hence a two tailed test. For this class, we will focus on two-tailed tests. This is not to say that one-tailed tests are not important, they are, but we will keep it simple. Furthermore, we want to achieve at least a 95% level of confidence that we can reject the hypothesis that the average wage is 6.5 ($\alpha = .05$).

To test a single parameter, in this case the mean, we use a t-test. To conduct a t-test you need to find the t-statistic, which is shown with the following equation:

$$t - stat = \frac{\hat{\beta} - \beta}{SE(\hat{\beta})}$$

This is the generic way to write a t-stat. It is important to note that β represents a population parameter. $\hat{\beta}$ is a sample parameter, that means it is estimated from the data.

When testing averages or means, we can write it out this way:

$$t - stat = \frac{Sample\ Mean - Population\ Mean}{SE(sample\ mean)} = \frac{\bar{x} - \mu}{SE(\bar{x})}$$

Your next question is probably going to be, what in tarnation is the standard error? I can answer that for you

$$SE(\hat{\beta}) = \frac{Std\ Dev\ (\hat{\beta})}{\sqrt{N}}$$

Now that we have that out of the way, let's calculate a t-stat.
Let's see if we can calculate this by hand using the wages.xlsx data set.

1. Mean

wage		
3	Mean	=AVERAGE(A2:A527)
6	Standard Deviation	AVERAGE(number1, [numb
5.3	N	
8.8	Standard Error	

2. Standard Deviation

wage		
3	Mean	5.908992395
6	Standard Deviation	=STDEV(A2:A527)
5.3	N	
8.8	Standard Error	

3. N

wage		
3	Mean	5.908992395
6	Standard Deviation	3.709104465
5.3	N	=COUNT(A2:A527)
8.8	Standard Error	
11	t-stat	

4. Standard Error

wage		
3	Mean	5.908992395
6	Standard Deviation	3.709104465
5.3	N	526
8.8	Standard Error	=D3/SQRT(D4)
11	t-stat	

5. T-stat (remember that our population mean comes from the question.

wage		
3	Mean	5.908992395
6	Standard Deviation	3.709104465
5.3	N	526
8.8	Standard Error	0.16172464
11	t-stat	=(D2-6.5)/D5

t-stat = -3.65

Now that we have a t-stat, how can we change this into a p-value so that we can reject or fail to reject our hypothesis? Is the difference statistically different? We have two approaches, first we could evaluate the critical t-statistic for the pre-determined levels of significance. For example, a sufficiently large sample (>120) will result in a t-statistic of 1.96 for the critical p-value of 0.05 (95% confidence). This method will be explained later on. Another method would be to calculate the p-value directly from the t-statistic in Excel. We can do this in the following way:

6. P-value

wage			
3.1	Mean	5.908992395	
3.2	Standard Deviation	3.709104465	
3	N	526	
6	Standard Error	0.16172464	
5.3	t-stat	-3.654406678	
8.8	p-value	=TDIST(D6,D4-1,2)	
11		TDIST(x, deg_freedom, **tails**)	

But, wait!! We have an error #NUM! The issue is that Excel does not like the negative t-stat. By putting a negative in front of the t-stat, we then generate our p-value, 0.00028. Armed with our p-value, we can now move forward and reject the null hypothesis and conclude that the mean of wages is not 6.5 because our p-value falls below the pre-determined significance threshold of 0.05.

Let's return now to comparing the t-stat and drawing conclusions.

Before any estimations, you need to choose your significance level (often times referred to as α). Based on that significance level, there is a corresponding critical value. See the graph below:

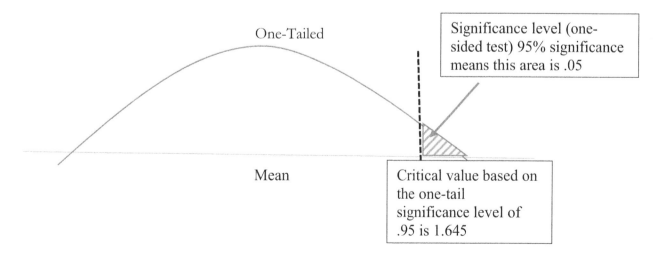

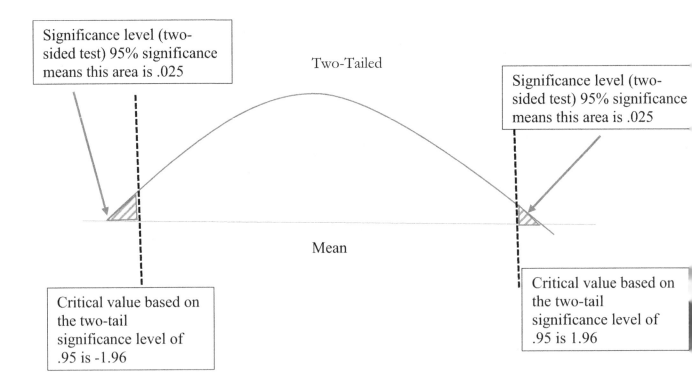

Significance level (two-sided test) 95% significance means this area is .025

Two-Tailed

Significance level (two-sided test) 95% significance means this area is .025

Mean

Critical value based on the two-tail significance level of .95 is -1.96

Critical value based on the two-tail significance level of .95 is 1.96

Just as there is a direct relationship between the critical value and the significance level, there is a direct relationship between the t-statistic and a p-value. These numbers come from estimating the null hypothesis.

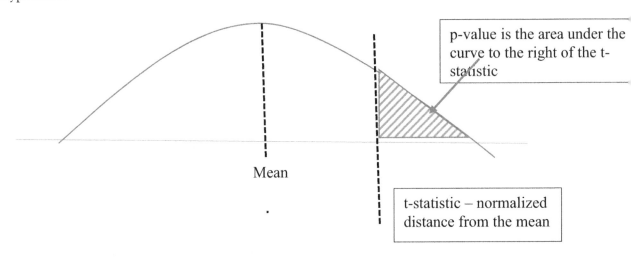

p-value is the area under the curve to the right of the t-statistic

Mean

t-statistic – normalized distance from the mean

Notice that as the t-stat gets larger, the p-value gets smaller

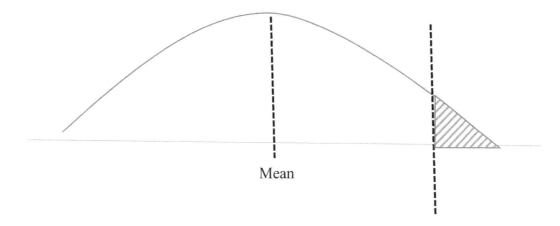

Mean

If you have additional questions on t-stat or p-value, consult your stats book. That class was a pre-requisite for this one (sorry to bring that up again)

So going back to the claim, wages are $6.50, is this true? Because we calculated a t-stat of -3.65, this value would fall to the left of the -1.96 (which is what we call the rejection region) and the p-value is less than 0.05. Thus, we reject the null and conclude that the sample mean is significantly different from 6.50.

Suppose for instance that instead of 6.50, we propose the null hypothesis is $H_o: \beta = 6$
Then calculating the t-stat we would find that it equals -0.56 and the corresponding p-value is above 0.05. This does not fall in either rejection region, and thus we would conclude that there is not statistical difference from the sample mean and the population mean.

See videos: https://www.youtube.com/watch?v=kAVZVg4rUdY
                https://www.youtube.com/watch?v=3RHQ1hlxDwk

Now that you know how to calculate the t-stat by hand, you are prepared to learn the short cut. You can run Descriptive Statistics on the variable of interest. Go to Data Analyis>Descriptive Statistics. For the Input Range select the variable of interest. If you select the entire column, make sure to click the Labels in First Row box, click on Summary Statistics. And then…BOOM. This will provide all the summary statistics you need to calculate a t-stat: mean and standard error. You can use this as a short cut to calculate the t-stat.

Example 5.4a   In other survey of workers in the US, the average years of work experience is 16 years. Using wages.xlsx, do you agree or disagree with this claim? Provide support for your answer.

Example 5.4b   An article you read says that the average worker has been at the job for 6 years. Is this statement true? Explain and provide support.

Solution Example 5.4a

Start with the Hypothesis:

$H_0: experience = 16$

$H_A: experience \neq 16$

$t - stat = \frac{17.02 - 16}{0.59} = 1.72$ and $p - value = 0.086$

We fail to reject the null hypothesis. This means that we do not have any evidence to disagree with this statement.

exper			
		Beta	16
Mean	17.01711027	t-stat	1.718747
Standard Error	0.59177428	p-value	0.08625

Solution Example 5.4b

Start with the hypothesis:

$H_0: tenure = 6$

$H_A: tenure \neq 6$

$t - stat = \frac{5.10 - 6}{0.32} = -2.843$ and $p - value = 0.005$

From this, we reject the null and conclude that the average worker has NOT been at their current job for 6 years (it is closer to 5 years).

tenure			
		Beta	6
Mean	5.104562738	t-stat	-2.84264
Standard Error	0.315001525	p-value	0.004648

Testing Two Parameters

Now that we have tested a population parameter is equal to a number, let's now look to see if we can compare two parameters to each other.

For example, let's test the difference to see if the wages for women are significantly different from wages for men. This is slightly different, because the test is not if the sample variable is equal to a population variable, but rather if a sample variable is equal to another sample variable.

So to restate that, do men and women make the same wages?

We formulate our null hypothesis

$$H_0: wages_{male} = wages_{females}$$

And our alternative hypothesis

$$H_A: wages_{male} \neq wages_{females}$$

If we find an example where wages for men and women are different, we can reject the null hypothesis and conclude that they do not make the same wages.

To test the hypothesis we can still use a t-stat. To do so, we need to rewrite the null hypothesis.

$$H_0: wages_{male} - wages_{females} = 0$$

And now we can use the following t-stat equation for testing two parameters:

$$t - stat = \frac{(\hat{\beta}_1 - \hat{\beta}_2) - (\beta_1 - \beta_2)}{SE(\hat{\beta}_1 - \hat{\beta}_2)}$$

It is important to note that $SE(\hat{\beta}_1 - \hat{\beta}_2) \neq SE(\hat{\beta}_1) - SE(\hat{\beta}_2)$

Calculating this hybrid standard error by hand is quite difficult and time consuming. Thankfully, there is a tool within excel to do this.

Applying the general t-stat formula, for our situation we can replace the values to produce the following:

$$t - stat = \frac{(\overline{wages}_{male} - \overline{wages}_{female}) - 0}{SE(\overline{wages}_{male} - \overline{wages}_{female})}$$

Within the Data Analysis Toolpak, there are three options for t-tests.

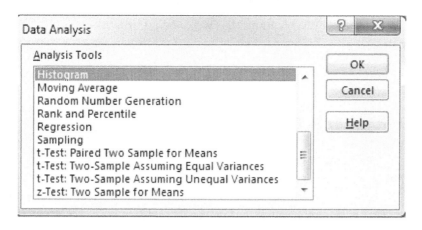

The first two t-Test options are for specific scenarios not covered in this class. We will choose the third option, t-Test: Two-Sample Assuming Unequal Variances. It is the least restrictive of the three options.

To test our claim we insert the wages for men for Variable 1 Range and the wages for women for Variable 2 Range. In this example, the data was sorted by gender and then the relevant ranges of wages was used.

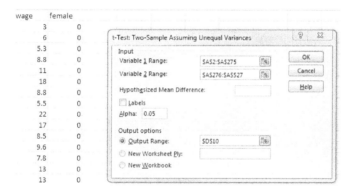

This gives us the following results

t-Test: Two-Sample Assuming Unequal Variances

	Variable 1	Variable 2
Mean	7.115328467	4.59734127
Variance	17.39785942	6.536904855
Observations	274	252
Hypothesized Mean Difference	0	
df	458	
t Stat	8.419716906	
P(T<=t) one-tail	2.44313E-16	
t Critical one-tail	1.648187415	
P(T<=t) two-tail	4.88627E-16	
t Critical two-tail	1.965157098	

This estimates our t-statistic = 8.42

Thus, our conclusion is that we reject the null. Meaning that we conclude that there is a difference in wages between males and females

If the t-stat was less than 1.96, then we would fail to reject the null and conclude that there is no statistically significant difference in wages between males and females

Another way to do the ttest is to use the ttest function within a cell.

Sort the data by gender, then go to an empty cell and use the command ttest:

=TTEST(*range of wage for men, range of wage for female, 2, 3*)

This test will return the p-value that is the probability that wages of males is equal to wages of females. This can be compared to your preselected significance level. You can now create a table to show all the relevant information needed to answer the question including a cell with the p-value.

Mean Wage of Males	Mean Wage of Females	Difference in Means
Standard Deviation	Standard deviation	=TTEST()

See the video: https://www.youtube.com/watch?v=pMkn00MWITA

Another way to test if men and women have the same wages is to filter the data for males, then copy and paste the column of wages into a new worksheet. Then go back to the original data and filter for females, copy and paste column of wages into that same worksheet. You can now use Data Analysis>t-test: Two-Sample Assuming Unequal Variance with this two columns as your variable ranges.

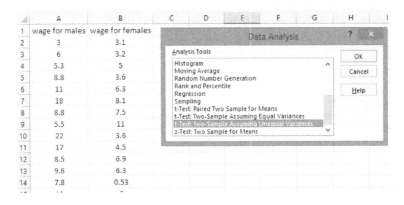

It will provide the same answer as using the sorting method.

Example 5.4c   Do individuals who are married have the same level of education as those who are not married?

Example 5.4d   Do individuals who are married have the same level of experience as those who are not married?

Solution Example 5.4c

H_O: $education_{married}$ − $education_{single}$ = 0

H_A: $education_{married}$ − $education_{single}$ ≠ 0

$t − stat = −1.56$

t-Test: Two-Sample Assuming Unequal Variances

	educ single	educ married
Mean	12.32524272	12.715625
Variance	7.498579209	7.740193966
Observations	206	320
Hypothesized Mean D	0	
df	442	
t Stat	-1.585963877	
P(T<=t) one-tail	0.056731315	
t Critical one-tail	1.648308349	
P(T<=t) two-tail	0.113462631	
t Critical two-tail	1.965345591	

We fail to reject the null. We conclude that educational levels is no different between those who are married and single.

Solution Example 5.4d

H_O: $experience_{married}$ − $experience_{single}$ = 0

H_A: $experience_{married}$ − $experience_{single}$ ≠ 0

$t − stat = −7.60$

t-Test: Two-Sample Assuming Unequal Variances

	exper single	exper married
Mean	11.66019417	20.465625
Variance	171.6303102	162.4000686
Observations	206	320
Hypothesized Mean Difference	0	
df	429	
t Stat	-7.604869394	

We reject the null and conclude that married individuals have higher levels of work experience than single individuals do.

Chapter 5.5 Types of Data Analysis

Now that you have all the tools, let's briefly summarize different types of data analysis. We previously mentioned that you can generally characterize data analysis into two categories – descriptive and causal. However, as data analysis has matured the categories of data analysis have become more granular. Below are the six generally accepted mutually exclusive types of data analysis popularized by Dr. Jeffrey Leek (link). Dr. Leek's explanations are summarized below.

Six Types of Analyses that Every Data Scientist Should Know
1. Descriptive
2. Exploratory
3. Inferential
4. Predictive
5. Causal
6. Mechanistic

1. Descriptive (least amount of effort): The discipline of quantitatively describing the main features of a collection of data. In essence, it describes a set of data.
- Typically, the first kind of data analysis performed on a data set
- Commonly applied to large volumes of data, such as census data
- The description and interpretation processes are different steps
- Univariate and Bivariate are two types of statistical descriptive analyses.
- *Type of data set applied to:* Census Data Set – a whole population

2. Exploratory: An approach to analyzing data sets to find previously unknown relationships.
- Exploratory models are good for discovering new connections
- They are also useful for defining future studies/questions
- Exploratory analyses are usually not the definitive answer to the question at hand, but only the start
- Exploratory analyses alone should not be used for generalizing and/or predicting
- Remember: correlation does not imply causation
- *Type of data set applied to:* Census and Convenience Sample Data Set (typically non-uniform) – a random sample with many variables measured

3. Inferential: Aims to test theories about the nature of the world in general (or some part of it) based on samples of "subjects" taken from the world (or some part of it). That is, use a relatively small sample of data to say something about a bigger population.
- Inference is commonly the goal of statistical models
- Inference involves estimating both the quantity you care about and your uncertainty about your estimate
- Inference depends heavily on both the population and the sampling scheme
- *Type of data set applied to:* Observational, Cross Sectional Time Study, and Retrospective Data Set – the right, randomly sampled population

4. Predictive: The various types of methods that analyze current and historical facts to make predictions about future events. In essence, to use the data on some objects to predict values for another object.

- The models predicts but it does not mean that the independent variables cause
- Accurate prediction depends heavily on measuring the right variables
- Although there are better and worse prediction models, more data and a simple model works really well
- Prediction is very hard, especially about the future references
- *Type of data set applied to:* Prediction Study Data Set – a training and test data set from the same population

5. Causal: To find out what happens to one variable when you change another.

- Implementation usually requires randomized studies
- There are approaches to inferring causation in non-randomized studies
- Causal models are said to be the "gold standard" for data analysis
- *Type of data set applied to:* Randomized Trial Data Set – data from a randomized study

6. Mechanistic (most amount of effort): Understand the exact changes in variables that lead to changes in other variables for individual objects.

- Incredibly hard to infer, except in simple situations
- Usually modeled by a deterministic set of equations (physical/engineering science)
- Generally, the random component of the data is measurement error
- If the equations are known but the parameters are not, they may be inferred with data analysis
- *Type of data set applied to:* Randomized Trial Data Set – data about all components of the system

Chapter 6
Regression Analysis

"Economics is totally un-useful. They teach us all about demand curves and how to use them but never teach us nothing on how to find a demand curve in real life."

This is a legitimate critique of principles of microeconomics. So let me satisfy that student who was left wanting after just one econ course. In this section, you will be able to estimate a demand curve. #yourewelcome #sorryitcamelate #itwasbetterforyourgradenottocoveritinaprinciplescourse

A demand curve is just a linear relationship between two variables. For example, you might have seen a demand curve that looks like this:

$$Quantity = 1,000 - 10P$$

This tells us the relationship between price and quantity. In this case, if price were to increase by \$1, then quantity would decrease by 10.

This looks a lot like $y = mx + b$. And this shows us that to be able to find the relationship between quantity and price, we just need an intercept (b) and a slope (m).

So if we wanted to do this in real life, we would look at data. Consider the 32 oz Diet Coke fountain drink (aka the elixir of the Gods). I can look at all the different places that sell this good in Cedar City and create a data set that has the price the store charges and how many sales they made at that price (quantity). I can then plot all those out on a scatter plot and it might look something like this:

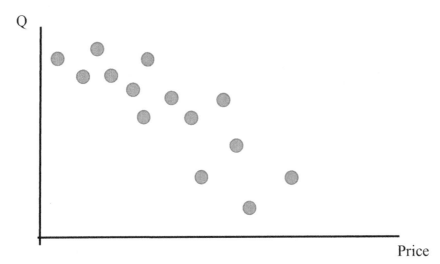

Each blue circle, represents a unit of observation, that is the price charged and the quantity sold at that price. Notice that you see a general downward trend, that is when the price was lower, a higher quantity was sold. As the price increased, the quantity demanded decreased.

What regression analysis will do is to use this data and create a best-fit line that best represents the relationship between quantity and price.

More generally, regression analysis can be used to estimate the relationship between many different variables. It is an incredibly useful tool for answering questions.

We want to fit a best-fit line to represent the data. Consider the following two best fit lines on the same figure:

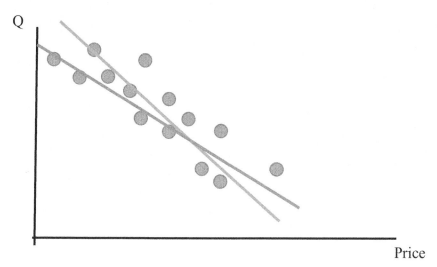

Which line best fits the data? Green or Red?

The eyeball test may not be sufficient to find that true relationship. The difference between the two lines, besides their color, is that they have a different intercept and a different slope. We need to choose an intercept and slope that best describes the relationship.

To do that we can rewrite the equation in a fancy way, or what we call an econometric model.

This formula might feel a little overwhelming at first. Let's walk through each part of it, beginning with our classic point-slope formula. Let's go through one-step at a time. Notice what changes between each step

1) $y = mx + b$
2) $y = b + mx$
3) $y = \beta_0 + mx$
4) $y = \beta_0 + \beta_1 x$
5) $y = \beta_0 + \beta_1 x_1$

The y is the result of the model. In our example above the price is the input, and as a result a certain quantity demanded occurs. β_0 is our y intercept. The x_1 is simply the first variable in our model, while the β_1 is our coefficient, or slope. Now you are ready for the big jump to the final steps.

$$Quantity = \beta_0 + \beta_1(Price)$$

We substituted the y for Quantity, and the x_1 for Price because in our situation we know what the y and x variables are. While we know that quantity is the y-variable, we need a new name for it. It prefers to be called the outcome or dependent variable, while the x variables are called choosing or

197

independent variables. Depending on your field of work, the y and x can actually take on a number of different names, but we'll stick with these few names for now.

$$\widehat{Quantity} = \hat{\beta}_0 + \hat{\beta}_1 (Price)_i$$

Sometimes we will have little hats on our coefficients. This means that we are generating estimates for these values based on a sample. Now that you have seen the hats, we are going to take them back off for the final tricky step.

$$Quantity_i = \beta_0 + \beta_1 (Price)_i + u_i$$

We have an added i subscript. (Subscript means the small letters next to the variable). Each i represents a dot, or an observation, on the graph. The graph above has 14 dots, so i goes from 1 to 14. Now, for any given price of the product we could use our formula to guess the quantity. That sure beats just randomly guessing an answer! However, is our guess going to be perfect? Usually not. Looking at the graph again and notice how with either of the two lines sometimes our guess (the line) is too high (above the point) or too low (below the point). The u_i is the measurement of how far off our lines is for any individual point. This u is referred to as either the error or residual, and is best represented as the distance from the point to the best fit line possible. Errors in our models are just fine. Because we do not have all of the information in the universe, our models and projections are not going to be perfectly accurate. For example, humans have been trying to predict the weather for thousands of years, and we are still struggling at it. That is okay.

Assume the red line is the best fit line:

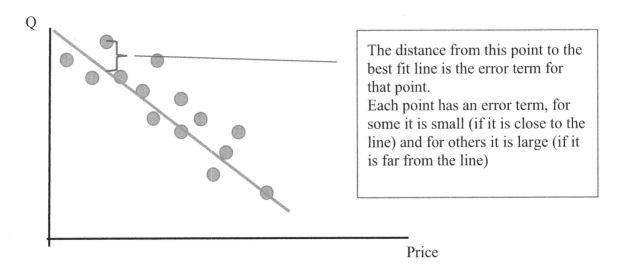

The distance from this point to the best fit line is the error term for that point.
Each point has an error term, for some it is small (if it is close to the line) and for others it is large (if it is far from the line)

The process to choose the best-fit line is to choose a line that minimizes the distance for all the lines. This process is called OLS (Ordinary Least Squares) or Sum of Squared Errors. In other words, OLS produces the line that minimizes the sum of all of the squared error terms. How can we minimize the sum of squared errors? You know how to minimize from our Calculus days together earlier in the textbook.

How to calculate the values for $\widehat{\beta}_0$ and $\widehat{\beta}_1$ by hand

Let's go back to the base example.
$$y_i = \beta_0 + \beta_1 x_i + u_i$$

We can rewrite this by rearranging the variables in the following way:
$$u_i = y_i - \beta_0 - \beta_1 x_i$$

That's the error term, now we just need to square it and then add it all up to create one number. This one number is the sum of squared error, and in some fields is referred to generally as the "loss."
$$\sum u_i^2 = \sum (y_i - \beta_0 + \beta_1 x_i)^2$$

There you have it, now we choose β_0 and β_1 to minimize the sum of squared errors.
$$Min \ \sum u_i^2 = \sum (y_i - \beta_0 + \beta_1 x_i)^2$$

Remember: to minimize a function, you take the first derivative and set it equal to zero. We will use that same strategy to minimize this function. Before we took the derivative with respect to x or to y. We did that to solve for x* and y*. In this case we are not solving for x and y, we are trying to find the β_0 and β_1 that create the best fit line. So we will take the first derivative with respect to β_0 and β_1.

We start with this $\quad Min \ \sum \hat{u}_i^2 = \sum (y_i - \hat{\beta}_0 - \hat{\beta}_1 x_i)^2$

We take a derivate with respect to $\hat{\beta}_0$ and $\hat{\beta}_1$. This will create one equation for each derivative

(i) $\quad \dfrac{\partial}{\partial \beta_0} = 2 \sum (y_i - \hat{\beta}_0 - \hat{\beta}_1 x_i)(-1) = 0$

(ii) $\quad \dfrac{\partial}{\partial \beta_1} = 2 \sum (y_i - \hat{\beta}_0 - \hat{\beta}_1 x_i)(-x_i) = 0$

Let's work with equation (i)
$$2 \sum (y_i - \hat{\beta}_0 - \hat{\beta}_1 x_i)(-1) = 0$$
Divide each side by -2
$$\sum (y_i - \hat{\beta}_0 - \hat{\beta}_1 x_i) = 0$$
Divide each side by $\frac{1}{n}$
$$\frac{1}{n} \sum (y_i - \hat{\beta}_0 - \hat{\beta}_1 x_i) = 0$$
Factor the $\frac{1}{n}$ through the equation
$$\frac{1}{n} \sum y_i - \frac{1}{n} \sum \hat{\beta}_0 - \frac{1}{n} \sum \hat{\beta}_1 x_i = 0$$
$$\bar{y} - \frac{1}{n} n \hat{\beta}_0 - \hat{\beta}_1 \bar{x} = 0$$
Solve for $\hat{\beta}_0$
$$\hat{\beta}_0 = \bar{y} - \hat{\beta}_1 \bar{x}$$

Now that we have solved for $\hat{\beta}_0$, we will need to use this with (ii) to solve for $\hat{\beta}_1$

From (ii), ley's divide each side by -2

$$\sum(y_i - \hat{\beta}_0 - \hat{\beta}_1 x_i)(x_i) = 0$$

Let's substitute $\hat{\beta}_0 = \bar{y} - \hat{\beta}_1\bar{x}$ in where we see $\hat{\beta}_0$

$$\frac{1}{n}\sum x_i(y_i - (\bar{y} - \hat{\beta}_1\bar{x}) - \hat{\beta}_1 x_i) = 0$$

$$\sum x_i(y_i - \bar{y}) = \hat{\beta}_1 \sum x_i(x_i - \bar{x})$$

solve for $\hat{\beta}_1$

$$\hat{\beta}_1 = \frac{\sum x_i(y_i - \bar{y})}{\sum x_i(x_i - \bar{x})}$$

This next step is a statistical magic trick, one that can be found in a stats textbook. But we can rewrite this equation in the following way

$$\hat{\beta}_1 = \frac{\sum(x_i - \bar{x})(y_i - \bar{y})}{\sum(x_i - \bar{x})^2}$$

You may not see it right away, but the numerator is the equation for the Cov (x,y) and the denominator is the equation for the Var (x). Thus $\hat{\beta}_1$ is the covariance of x and y divided by the variance of x.

So $\hat{\beta}_1 = \frac{Cov(x,y)}{var(x)}$

Now that we have solved for $\hat{\beta}_0$ and $\hat{\beta}_1$, let's take a step back and see what we have done. We are trying to find the best fit line that will represent the relationship between x and y. This line will have two parts: the y-intercept ($\hat{\beta}_0$) and a slope ($\hat{\beta}_1$). To find these two values, we use the equation of the line and minimize the sum of squared errors. We take derivatives of the equation and solve for $\hat{\beta}_0$ and $\hat{\beta}_1$. So doing yields the following two results:

$$\hat{\beta}_0 = \bar{y} - \hat{\beta}_1\bar{x}$$

$$\hat{\beta}_1 = \frac{\sum(x_i - \bar{x})(y_i - \bar{y})}{\sum(x_i - \bar{x})^2}$$

The key is not to memorize this equation, but to realize that when we estimate models in Excel, this is exactly what Excel is doing.

Now that we know how to estimate the best fit line, let's return back to our example.

Example 6.1a   **Given the following model or quantity and price:**
$$Quantity_i = \beta_0 + \beta_1(Price)_i + u_i$$

What is β_0?

> [ ]

What is β_1?

> [ ]

Interpret is β_0?

> [ ]

Interpret is β_1?

> [ ]

Stop! Do not keep reading unless you actually write something into those boxes. How are you gonna learn if you don't write it down?

Solutions Example 6.1a

What is β_0?

The intercept for Quantity

What is β_1?

The slope

Now let's look at the more challenging ones:

Interpret is β_0?

The average quantity demanded when price is 0

Interpret is β_1?

The change in quantity demanded for a unit change in price Or The Δ in quantity demanded for a unit Δ in price

Based on these interpretations, what does economic theory tell us about the sign of β_1?

Stop!! Again, why did I go through all that trouble for you to not actually answer the question?

If you were to answer the question, economic theory would suggest that β_1 is negative, that is a change in the price leads to a decrease in the quantity demanded. That is theory, now let's use data to answer the question, that is, to empirically estimate the model.

Let's use data set smoking, to see the relationship between the price of cigarettes and quantity demanded. The price of cigarettes is measured in cents per pack and the quantity is measured as cigarettes smoked per day.

One way to estimate this model is to do so graphically.
In Excel, go to the ribbon and click on Insert.

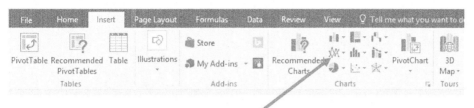

We are going to create a scatter chart, which is the top left option of scatter charts. This will create a blank white box. Right click on that box and choose "Select Data"
Add a Series, this will allow you to select your y and x variables. In your model, your x variable is price (cigpric) and y variable is quantity (cigs). I did not highlight the label of the row.

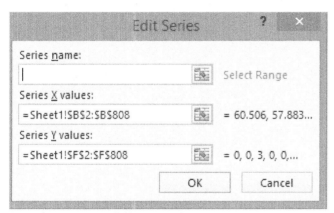

This should create the following chart:

This is the data plotted out.

Of all of the blue points on the graph, left-click your favorite one, and then right-click on it, and then click on Add Trendline.

This will open a new window, Linear is the default option, keep that, and then click on display Equation on chart.

This will give you the equation of the best-fit line. Which looks like this: y = -0.033x + 10.675
This tells us that

$$\hat{\beta}_0 = 10.675$$
$$\hat{\beta}_1 = -0.033$$

Ouila!! We have just estimated the coefficients which gives us the best-fit line!!!

Estimating OLS in Excel

Now, this was not the most efficient or best way to generate a least squares equation, but it is a clear graphical approach. Let's begin to use more sophisticated tools.

Go to Data > Data Analysis > Regression. (Remember, if you do not have Data Analysis installed on Excel, you can turn it on within the file options.)

The steps above will open the following box:

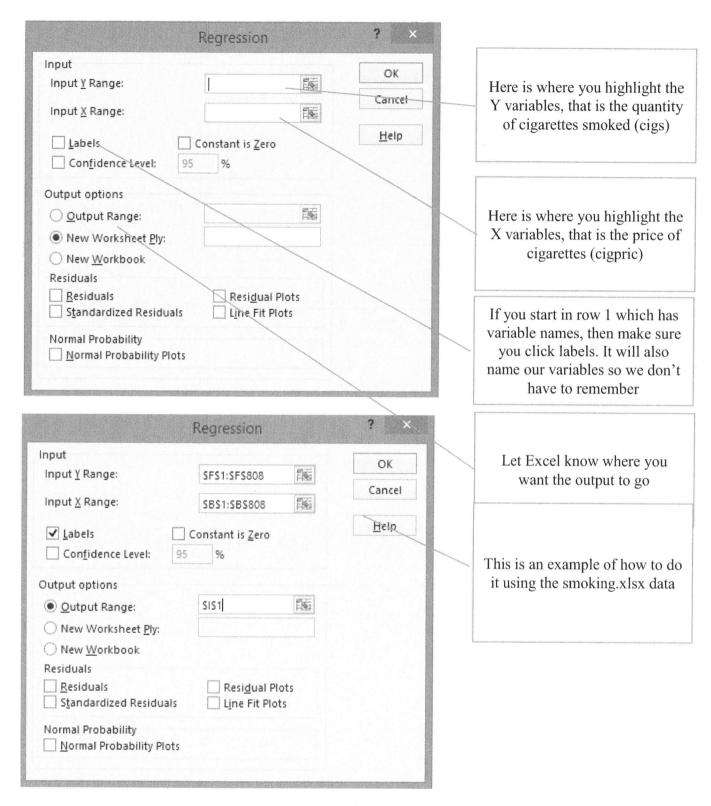

Here is where you highlight the Y variables, that is the quantity of cigarettes smoked (cigs)

Here is where you highlight the X variables, that is the price of cigarettes (cigpric)

If you start in row 1 which has variable names, then make sure you click labels. It will also name our variables so we don't have to remember

Let Excel know where you want the output to go

This is an example of how to do it using the smoking.xlsx data

If you have performed the steps above correctly, you will see the following output from Excel.

SUMMARY OUTPUT

Regression Statistics	
Multiple R	0.011385433
R Square	0.000129628
Adjusted R Square	-0.001112447
Standard Error	13.72914618
Observations	807

ANOVA

	df	SS	MS	F	Significance F
Regression	1	19.67153752	19.67153752	0.104364128	0.74673796
Residual	805	151734.0112	188.489455		
Total	806	151753.6828			

	Coefficients	Standard Error	t Stat	P-value	Lower 95%	Upper 95%
Intercept	10.67457339	6.172958875	1.72924745	0.08414818	-1.442421817	22.7915686
cigpric	-0.032969596	0.102055873	-0.323054372	0.74673796	-0.233296628	0.167357436

Notice that Excel does not give the names $\hat{\beta}_0$ or $\hat{\beta}_1$. Instead it provides the coefficients of the intercept ($\hat{\beta}_0$) and the coefficient on the variable cigpric ($\hat{\beta}_1$).

Now let's interpret these two coefficients $\hat{\beta}_0$ and $\hat{\beta}_1$. The interpretation does not really change from before, except when you have a hat, you have a number.

Interpret $\hat{\beta}_0$: the average number of cigarettes demanded when the price is zero is 10.67
Interpret $\hat{\beta}_1$: the change in cigarettes demanded for a unit change in price (one cent) is -0.033

All that we have to do is take the interpretation from the model and add a number. Kind of like Beyonce's if you like it then you better put a ring on it, but more like if you estimate it then you better put a hat on it.

Let's use our output in the context of our previous graph and equations to see what we have actually done. We have estimated the line that best fits the data.

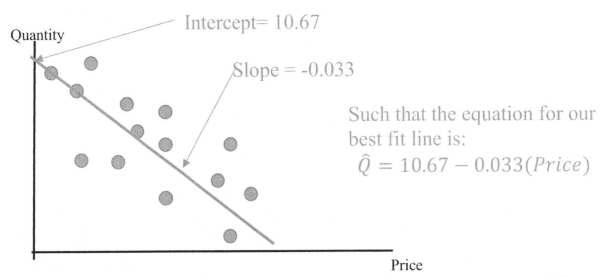

This means that if you input a price, the function will give you an estimated quantity. So if the price of cigarettes were to be 60.506 cents, we would put that into price

$$\hat{Q} = 10.67 - 0.033(60.506) = 8.67$$

Our model would predict that the demand would be 8.67 cigarettes per day, on average. This does not mean that everyone will smoke that much. What it does mean is that at the 60.506 cents price, the expected (or average) demand is 8.67 cigarettes. For example, look at the first observation in the data set. That individual could have bought cigarettes at 60.506 cents, but did not buy any. This means that the error term for that one person ($\hat{u}_1$) is -8.67.

Example 6.1c   **It is argued that with the increasing population in Cedar City, crime is increasing as a result. We want to test this claim.**

We need to create a model to test this claim.

What is the outcome about which we are concerned? In this case it is crime. So crime will be our outcome or dependent variable (left hand side variable or y variable). What is the changing variable? In this case it is population. So our model will look like the equation below. (Crime is number of crimes and population is number of people.)

Model of Crime and Population:
$$crime = \beta_0 + \beta_1(population) + u$$

Interpret is β_0?

```



```

Interpret is β_1?

```



```

β_0 is the expected number of crimes when population is 0

β_1 is the change in the number of crimes for a change in the population. This is, crime will increase by β_1 for each additional person added to the population.

It is useful to point out that, β_0 may not always have a meaningful interpretation. Like in this case, it may not be too meaningful as there are no cities with zero people. Graphically it might look like this:

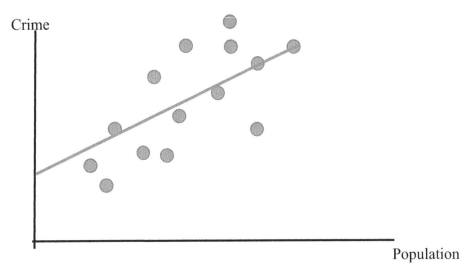

Crime

Population

Notice that the intercept is different from zero on this graph, so this would indicate that the average crime with no population is different from zero. But also notice that there are no observations with zero population, so while we can interpret β_0, it may not be the most meaningful interpretation, as it is outside the existing and feasible region of our data.

Now let's turn to β_1, this is interpreted as the change in crime for each unit change of population, or in other words, the change in the number of crimes for an increase of population by one person. This number could be positive, negative or zero.

Notice that β_1 is related to the argument that was made. So let's set up our hypothesis.

$H_o: \beta_1 = 0$
$H_A: \beta_1 \neq 0$

Why is this the hypothesis that addresses the argument? Suppose the Null hypothesis is true, then β_1 is zero. That means that the change in the number of crimes for a change in population is zero. That is, increasing population has no effect on crime.

Suppose the alternative hypothesis is true, then β_1 is not zero, meaning that a change in the population changes the number of crimes.

Based on that hypothesis, we can perform a t-test.

$$t - stat = \frac{\hat{\beta}_1 - \beta_1}{SE(\hat{\beta}_1)}$$

β_1 comes from our hypothesis and $\hat{\beta}_1$ comes from data.

But before we look at the data, let's look at what will happen once we do.
Based on our t-test, we will get a t-stat that falls into one of several areas based on a 95% confidence interval ($\alpha=.05$):

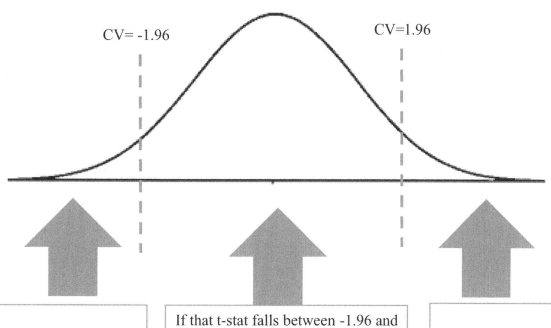

If the t-stat is less than -1.96, the it falls in rejection region. This means that we reject the null, and conclude that an increase in population leads to a decrease in crime

If that t-stat falls between -1.96 and 1.96, then we fail to reject the null hypothesis. This means that we don't reject the null, meaning that we have no evidence to suggest that the relationship is different from zero. This means that there is no statistical relationship between population and crime, and we dismiss the claim.

If the t-stat is greater than 1.96, the it falls in rejection region. This means that we reject the null, and conclude that an increase in population leads to an increase in crime

It is important to note that we have gone through the whole process of testing the claim without using data. I encourage you to go through this process to make sure you understand what you are doing and why you are doing it. We are going to the data in order to test this claim. And, based on the data, you can test the claim based on the estimated coefficient ($\hat{\beta}_1$)

Estimating Example 6.1c
Now let's turn to the data, the file crime2.xlsx is what we will use here. These data come from the early 80's and contains information on the number of crimes and the number of people in the city. Let's estimate the regression model using Data Analysis>Regression

Without modifying the data, you can fill out the Regression box as follows:

The Excel output should look like this:

SUMMARY OUTPUT

Regression Statistics	
Multiple R	0.890094313
R Square	0.792267885
Adjusted R Square	0.789959751
Standard Error	13607.93399
Observations	92

ANOVA

	df	SS	MS	F	Significance F
Regression	1	63561671144	63561671144	343.250295	1.82226E-32
Residual	90	16665828075	185175867.5		
Total	91	80227499219			

	Coefficients	Standard Error	t Stat	P-value	Lower 95%	Upper 95%
Intercept	-1632.085174	2642.150197	-0.617710975	0.538325765	-6881.177704	3617.007356
pop	0.104423927	0.005636306	18.52701527	1.82226E-32	0.093226421	0.115621432

From this we know that
$$\hat{\beta}_0 = -1632$$
$$\hat{\beta}_1 = 0.104$$
Now for the interpretation

$\hat{\beta}_1$ is the change in the number of crimes for a unit change in population which is .104. That is for each increase in person in the city, the number of crimes will increase by .104. Thus if the population increases by 10 people, you would multiply 10 by .104 and would expect crime to increase by 1.04 incidents of crime.

Now for our hypothesis test

Excel Regression output provides not just the coefficient ($\hat{\beta}_1$) but also the standard error and the t-stat. In this case the t-stat is 18.53. This falls far to the right of our critical value and into the rejection region. Also, the p-value is provided to help us identify the rejection region. This number is in scientific notation, but this essentially means that the p-value is very close to zero and is below our significance threshold of 0.05. Therefore, we would reject the null hypothesis and conclude that an increase in population leads to a statistically significant increase in crime.

Example 6.1d   **We want to answer a question similar to that in Example 2, only that we want to know the relationship between police officers and the number of crimes.**

1. Write out the model that can find the relationship between police officers and crime.
2. Write out the hypothesis to test this
3. Estimate your model in Excel.
4. Interpret your model and how it relates to the scenario at hand.

Solution Example 6.1d

Model	$crime = \beta_0 + \beta_1(police\ officers) + u$

Hypothesis:
$H_0: \beta_1 = 0$
$H_A: \beta_1 \neq 0$

SUMMARY OUTPUT

Regression Statistics	
Multiple R	0.864896162
R Square	0.748045371
Adjusted R Square	0.745245875
Standard Error	14986.54574
Observations	92

ANOVA

	df	SS	MS	F	gnificance F
Regression	1	60013809431	60013809431	267.2072	1.11E-28
Residual	90	20213689788	224596553.2		
Total	91	80227499219			

	Coefficients	Standard Error	t Stat	P-value	Lower 95%	Upper 95%
Intercept	8831.457332	2449.258922	3.605767138	0.00051	3965.577	13697.34
police officers	33.39987195	2.043246426	16.34647272	1.11E-28	29.34061	37.45914

Excel output

$\hat{\beta}_1$ tells that the change in crime for each additional police officer is 33.4 incidents of crime. The t-stat is greater than 1.96, so we would reject the null and conclude that there is a statistically significant relationship between police officers and crime.

This shows that as you get more police officers, crime also increases.

It is important to note that this is not a causal relationship. It is a correlation. And indeed might be driven by other factors, such as population. As population increases, crime increases and police officers increase. Thus it may be the case that population is the reason behind the positive relationship between number of police officers and number of crimes.

This suggests that we might want to control for population when estimating our model. That leads us to discuss a multivariate model (one with multiple variables) than a single variable model.

Chapter 6.2 Multivariate Models

This is a fancy way of saying that we will have more than one variable in our model. Let's start with a generic model and then look at the example of crime.

Base model
$$y = \beta_0 + \beta_1 x_1 + \beta_2 x_2 + u$$

Let's look at interpretations.
β_0 is the average y when all x's are zero. Notice this is similar to what we had before, but instead of when x is zero, it is when all x's are zero.

β_1 is the change in y for a unit change in x_1, controlling for x_2. Again, it is similar to what we had before, except that is we have to acknowledge that there are other variables in the model that we are controlling for.

β_2 is the change in y for a unit change in x_2, controlling for x_1.

Now, let's look at the example of crime. Here is our model:

$$crime = \beta_0 + \beta_1(police\ officers) + \beta_2(population) + u$$

Interpretation time:
β_0 is the average number of crimes for a city with no police officers and no population (all x's are equal to zero). This is not meaningful as we don't have any cities with zero population, but that does not change the interpretation.

β_1 is the change in the number of crimes for each additional police officer, controlling for the city's population. The thought process here is to compare two cities with the same population, and then look to see the change in crime rate of a city with one more police officer than another city.

β_2 is the change in the number of crimes for each additional change in city population (+ 1 person in the population), controlling for the number of police officers.

Example 6.2a   **Estimate the following model and then**
1. Interpret each coefficient
2. Discuss the statistical significance of each coefficient

$$crime = \beta_0 + \beta_1(police\ officers) + \beta_2(population) + u$$

Solution Example 6.2a

This is the Excel spreadsheet and what you would input into Data Anlaysis>Regression

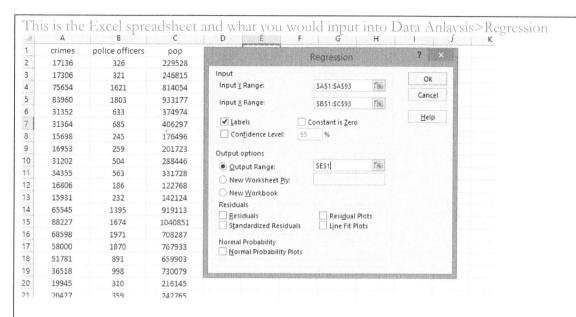

Once you click OK, you will get the following output:

SUMMARY OUTPUT

Regression Statistics	
Multiple R	0.909
R Square	0.826
Adjusted R Square	0.822
Standard Error	12511
Observations	92.000

ANOVA

	df	SS	MS	F	Significance F
Regression	2	6.6298E+10	3.31E+10	211.795	1.4557E-34
Residual	89	1.393E+10	1.57E+08		
Total	91	8.0227E+10			

	Coefficients	Standard Error	t Stat	P-value	Lower 95%	Upper 95%
Intercept	111.415	2464.613	0.045	0.964	-4785.718	5008.549
police officers	14.415	3.448	4.181	0.000	7.565	21.265
pop	0.066	0.010	6.336	0.000	0.046	0.087

Interpretation of the coefficients:

$\hat{\beta}_0$ - the average number of crimes in a city with zero police officers and no population is 111.415. **notice we don't add all else held constant, because all else is not just held constant but held constant at zero.

$\hat{\beta}_1$ – the change in the number of crimes for a unit change in police officers is 14.415 controlling for population.

$\hat{\beta}_2$ - the change in the number of crimes for a unit change in population is 0.066, controlling for the number of police officers. **notice that if you increase the number of people in the population by 1,000, it is expected that the number of crimes would increase by 66 incidents. If you divide 1 by 0.066, you get 15.15. So that means if you increase population by 15.15, the number of crimes would increase by 1.

Discussion of the statistical significance of the coefficients

Let's start with $\hat{\beta}_0$, is this number statistically different from zero? Well the null hypothesis is that $H_0: \hat{\beta}_0 = 0$. Based on the t-stat of the coefficient (.045) we would fail to reject the null hypothesis. Meaning that there is no evidence to suggest otherwise, and we conclude that the average number of crimes when there are no police officers or people is not different from zero. This number is a bit nonsensical, but that is okay. Mathematically, we must have an intercept. If there are no data points around the intercept, we do not need to worry about the p-value or t-stat.

Does an increase in police officers affect the number of crimes? This null hypothesis would be $H_0: \hat{\beta}_1 = 0$. Testing this hypothesis, we get the t-stat of 4.181 and a p-value of approximately 0, meaning that we reject the null and conclude that there is a statistically significant relationship between police officers and the number of crimes.

We have a similar conclusion when looking at the relationship between population and crime. We reject the null that there is no relationship, and conclude that increases in population lead to increases in crime. Conversely, a decrease in the population would lead to a decrease in the number of crimes.

All that we have discussed is applicable when our x-variables are quantitative data, that is when it is count data. What is count data, it is data you can count. You know, 1,2,3,4 – kind of like the way you can count the number of police officers or the number of people living in a city.

But, what do you do when you don't have a count variable? For example, what if you are considering purchasing different styles or types of homes? One of the most desirable homes to own, or so I am told, is a colonial home. Below is an image of a colonial home. Doesn't it look nice?

We can use data to show the difference in home prices between colonial and non-colonial homes. Use the data set hprice1.xlsx for this next section.

Using the data set, fill in the following table:

Average home price of a colonial home	Average home price of a non-colonial home

Notice how the table is blank, turn to Excel and estimate that table.

First, notice that the home price is in thousands of dollars, we need to convert it to dollars. Here is how you can do that:

	A	B
1	price	price$
2	300	=A2*1000
3	370	370000

There are a number of ways to find the average price of a colonial and non-colonial home. One is the AVERAGEIF command, like the following:

Colonial
=AVERAGEIF(G:G,1,B:B)

M	N	O
Colonial	Non-Colonial	
302918.869	=AVERAGEIF(G:G,0,B:B)	

This allows us to fill in the table accordingly,

Average home price of a colonial home	Average home price of a non-colonial home
$302,919	$272,370

What is the difference in average home prices? Colonial homes sell for an average of $30,548.50 more than colonial. Keep that number in mind: $30,548.50.

How then do we incorporate the qualitative data (like if the home is colonial) in our model? The first step is to convert the qualitative data into quantitative data. Let's create a variable, call it colonial. It is created in the following way:

$colonial = 1$ *if home is colonial*
$colonial = 0$ *if home is not colonial*

Notice that the new variable takes on two values, a zero or a one. As a result, it is called a binary or dummy variable. We can include it in our model just like we did with other variables. In the following way:

$$price = \beta_0 + \beta_1(colonial) + u$$

Before we turn to interpreting this, go ahead and estimate it and see if you can figure out the interpretation on your own.

This is how you would input the data into Data Analysis>Regression

	A	B	C	D	E	F	G	H	I	J	K
1	price$	colonial						Regression		?	×
2	300000	1			Input					OK	
3	370000	1			Input Y Range:			$A$1:$A$89			
4	191000	0								Cancel	
5	195000	1			Input X Range:			$B$1:$B$89			
6	373000	1								Help	
7	466275	1			☑ Labels		☐ Constant is Zero				
8	332500	1			☐ Confidence Level:		95	%			
9	315000	1			Output options						
10	206000	0			◉ Output Range:			$D$1			
11	240000	0			○ New Worksheet Ply:						
12	285000	1			○ New Workbook						
13	300000	1			Residuals						
14	405000	1			☐ Residuals		☐ Residual Plots				
15	212000	0			☐ Standardized Residuals		☐ Line Fit Plots				
16	265000	1			Normal Probability						
17	227400	1			☐ Normal Probability Plots						
18	240000	0									
19	285000	1									

Which yields the following output:

SUMMARY OUTPUT						
Regression Statistics						
Multiple R	0.137945777					
R Square	0.019029037					
Adjusted R Square	0.007622398					
Standard Error	102321.235					
Observations	88					
ANOVA						
	df	*SS*	*MS*	*F*	*gnificance F*	
Regression	1	1.75E+10	1.75E+10	1.668242	0.199955	
Residual	86	9E+11	1.05E+10			
Total	87	9.18E+11				
	Coefficients	*andard Err*	*t Stat*	*P-value*	*Lower 95%*	*Upper 95%*
Intercept	272370	19692	13.83171	1.4E-23	233224.5	311516.2
colonial	30548	23652	1.291605	0.199955	-16469.3	77566.3

Seeing the coefficients, can you figure out the interpretation of the coefficients of a dummy variable?

$\hat{\beta}_0$ is the average y when x is zero, in this case, it is the average home price when colonial is zero. Or in other words, the average home price of a non-colonial home is $272,370.

$\hat{\beta}_1$ is $30,548. This is the difference in average home price of colonial homes compared to non-colonial homes. And that is how you would interpret it, the change in average home price of a colonial home compared to a non-colonial home.

More generally,
The coefficient on a dummy variable is interpreted as the average difference in y for when x equals one compared to when x equals 0.

Omitted category – notice that the model has only one dummy variable. We do not use a dummy variable for both colonial house and non-colonial house. The omitted variable, in this case – the non-colonial house, is represented in the intercept or β_0. If we do not omit a category we create an unsolvable math problem. We will not work out by hand on how it becomes unsolvable. Believe me, it does not work.

Let me illustrate, consider the following model:

$$price = \beta_0 + \beta_1(colonial) + \beta_2(non - colonial) + u$$

Let's interpret β_0 – the average home price when the home is not colonial and when then home is not non-colonial. This is problematic because it is just not possible to have a home that is neither colonial or non-colonial. That is called the dummy variable trap ([link about a trap](#)). So the correct model will have one dummy variable for each binary quantitative variable.

Categorical Variables

Now instead of a qualitative variable like colonial, which is either yes or no, what if we had a variable that comes in categories. For example, suppose the data had several options for the respondent to fill in. The question on the survey where the data comes from might look like this:

What is the style of the home?
- o   Ranch
- o   Colonial
- o   Contemporary
- o   other

As a result, the data will show up in the following way:

Home Type
Ranch
Colonial
Contemporary
Contemporary
Ranch
Other
Contemporary
Ranch
Other

To convert that into quantitative data, it is necessary to create a dummy variable for each category. That is, convert it in the following way (in Excel):

	A	B	C	D	E
1	Home Type	Ranch	Colonial	Contemporary	Other
2	Ranch	=IF(A2="Ranch",1,0)		0	0
3	Colonial	0	1	0	0
4	Contemporary	0	0	1	0
5	Contemporary	0	0	1	0
6	Ranch	1	0	0	0
7	Other	0	0	0	1
8	Contemporary	0	0	1	0
9	Ranch	1	0	0	0
10	Other	0	0	0	1

For the next column you would do the following:

	A	B	C	D	E
1	Home Type	Ranch	Colonial	Contemporary	Other
2	Ranch	1	=IF(A2="Colonial",1,0)		0
3	Colonial	0	1	0	0
4	Contemporary	0	0	1	0
5	Contemporary	0	0	1	0
6	Ranch	1	0	0	0
7	Other	0	0	0	1
8	Contemporary	0	0	1	0
9	Ranch	1	0	0	0
10	Other	0	0	0	1

You would do the same for each column.

Consider the following model:
$$price = \beta_0 + \beta_1(colonial) + \beta_2(contemporary) + \beta_3(other) + u$$

Let's go through the interpretation of each coefficient.

β_0 is the average home price when x's are zero. That is it is the average home price when the home is not colonial, not contemporary and not other. So what is it?

You may have been asking, why didn't we include ranch as a variable in our model. That is because we omitted it. And β_0 is the average home price of the omitted category, that is it is the average home price of a ranch style home. Just like with a single dummy variable, categorical dummy variables also need an omitted category.

β_1 is the average change in home price of a colonial home compared to the omitted category, in this case compared to a ranch home

β_2 is the average change in home price of a contemporary home compared to a ranch home

With any type of dummy variable, the interpretation is always <u>compared to</u> the omitted category.

Homes vary in price and there are many reasons why the price varies. Think about what factors affect the home price: location, size of the home, the yard, location, number of bedrooms and baths, features, location, year built, and of course location. Let's look at a basic question, how much of the variation in home prices is explained by the type of home that it is: colonial or non-colonial?

First we refer to the model that we had before: $price = \beta_0 + \beta_1(colonial) + u$

The only variable in the model is a dummy variable for colonial home. We estimate the model and show the following output:

SUMMARY OUTPUT

Regression Statistics	
Multiple R	0.137945777
R Square	0.019029037
Adjusted R Square	0.007622398
Standard Error	102321.235
Observations	88

ANOVA

	df	SS	MS	F	gnificance F
Regression	1	1.75E+10	1.75E+10	1.668242	0.199955
Residual	86	9E+11	1.05E+10		
Total	87	9.18E+11			

	Coefficients	andard Err	t Stat	P-value	Lower 95%	Upper 95%
Intercept	272370	19692	13.83171	1.4E-23	233224.5	311516.2
colonial	30548	23652	1.291605	0.199955	-16469.3	77566.3

We are now going to focus on the R-squared. The interpretation of the R-squared is **how much of the variation of y is explained by the model (the x's)**. In this case we see that the R-squared is 0.019. The interpretation is as follows: 1.9 percent of the variation of home prices is explained by whether the home is colonial or not. The other 98.1 percent of why homes vary in price is due to other factors, like those we discussed above.

What do we mean when we say that a certain percentage of the variance is explained by the model? I am glad you asked such an insightful question. Imagine we have two people that are trying to guess the price of a home. One of these two people guesses the average home price for each person in the dataset. The second of these two people uses the information available (in this case whether the home is a colonial home) to make a more informed estimate of the home price. How much closer is the "informed" estimate over simply guessing the average over and over in terms of variance (or squared residual)? In this case, the informed guess has 1.9% lower variance. Or, we could say the model explains 1.9% of the variation in home prices.

So what happens when more variables are added to the model?

Let's use the following model:

$$price = \beta_0 + \beta_1(bedrooms) + \beta_2(lotsize) + \beta_3(sqrft) + \beta_4(colonial) + u$$

In this model, price is the price of the home in dollars, bedrooms is the number of bedrooms in the house, lotsize of size of the lot measured in square feet, sqrft is the size of the home measured in square feet, and colonial is a dummy variable which equals one if the home is a dummy variable.

Estimating the model provides the following:

SUMMARY OUTPUT					
Regression Statistics					
Multiple R	0.822065626				
R Square	0.675791894				
Adjusted R Square	0.660167407				
Standard Error	59876.96943				
Observations	88				
ANOVA					
	df	*SS*	*MS*	*F*	*gnificance F*
Regression	4	6.20279E+11	1.5507E+11	43.25210113	1.45E-19
Residual	83	2.97576E+11	3585251469		
Total	87	9.17855E+11			
	Coefficients	*Standard Error*	*t Stat*	*P-value*	*Lower 95%* *Upper 95%*
Intercept	-24127	29603	-0.814990313	0.417410278	-83006.6 34753.55
bdrms	11004	9515	1.156488822	0.250799111	-7921.18 29929.76
lotsize	2.08	0.64	3.230108205	0.001774189	0.797625 3.35404
sqrft	124.24	13.34	9.314369972	1.53438E-14	97.70822 150.7667
colonial	13716	14637	0.93702901	0.351462214	-15397.4 42828.47

Let's first focus on the R-squared. The model describes 67.6 percent of the variation in home prices. What describes the other 22.4 percent? Factors like location, features of the kitchen, age of the home, neighborhood, and location.

Using our example previously, let's imagine there are two people who are trying to guess the price of a home. The first of these people we will call Average Joe. Average Joe simply guesses the average for every home with a value of $293,546. We can then calculate how far off every guess is, square each one of those numbers, then add them up to come up with a single number for our level of "wrongness". (This is the formula for variance.) If you're curious, this number is actually in the regression output above. In the ANOVA table the Total row and SS column show a value of 9.17855E+11. The total wrongness is quite far off.

All right, now consider person two. This second person we will call Econometric Emily. Instead of just guessing the average, she uses the econometric formula below, which was created using the regression coefficients derived from the regression output above.

$$price = -24{,}127 + 11{,}004(bedrooms) + 2.08(lotsize) + 124.24(sqrft)$$
$$+ 13{,}716(colonial)$$

Emily uses this equation to estimate the home price for each home. We can then calculate how far off Emily is on each guess, square each one of these numbers, and add them up to come up with a single number for Emily's level of wrongness. This number is also in the ANOVA table. It is found in the row Residual and column SS. The number is 2.97576E+11. Average Joe's variance was about 9.2, while Emily's variance was about 3. That's a 67.6% improvement! In fact this is how R-Squared is calculated. The R-Squared is the percentage of variance explained by the model, or how much better Econometric Emily's guesses are than Average Joe's.

When does R-squared matter?

It matters most when predicting y is important. For example, let's look at the following data graphed out:

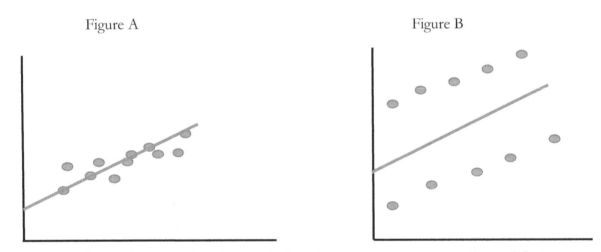

Figure A   Figure B

Let's compare the line in Figure A and Figure B. It is the exact same line, same β_0 and β_1. But notice that there is an important difference between the two, in Figure A, notice how the data points are all close to the line. This tells us that the model describes the data quite well. In this case, the R-squared would be closer to 1. In Figure B, there are no data points on the line, most are further from the line than in Figure A. In this case, the R-squared will be much smaller and closer to 0.

Suppose that both of these figures graphed the relationship between stock prices on the y-axis and time on the x-axis. Let's suppose you want to predict the stock price for the next day. The best fit line will let you plug in the next day's date and come up with a predicted stock price. Both models will provide the same stock price. But in Figure A, the predicted stock price is more likely to be accurate. In Figure B, the predicted stock price will be on the red line, but no previous stock prices are actually on the red line.

Thus when using the model to make predictions, a high R-squared is important.

The results of the last model we estimated showed that an additional bedroom increased the home price by $11,000 (we are ignoring the statistical significance at this time). But the question you should be able to answer is whether $11,000 is a big or small change. That all depends on the base price of the home. For a $100,000 home, that represents an 11 percent increase. For a $1 million home, that represents a 1.1% increase.

There is a way to take away the units and just use percent changes in our model. To do that we can use natural logs.

Our outcome variable has been price, so instead of price, let's now take the natural log of price and make that the dependent variable. To do that, go to Excel and take the natural log of price.

	A	B	C
1	price	price$	ln(price)
2	300	300000	=LN(B2)
3	370	370000	12.82126
4	191	191000	12.16003
5	195	195000	12.18075

The new model is as follows:

$$\ln(price) = \beta_0 + \beta_1(bedrooms) + \beta_2(lotsize) + \beta_3(sqrft) + \beta_4(colonial) + u$$

You can consider this a **"Log-Level" model**. A Log-Level model has a logged outcome and the X variables are normal units. To interpret this you should consider an additional unit of the X variable leads $(100 \times \beta)$ percentage change in the Y variable. Let's run a regression and see what happens with an example.

When we run a regression, we see the following results:

SUMMARY OUTPUT

Regression Statistics	
Multiple R	0.797577
R Square	0.636129
Adjusted R Square	0.618593
Standard Error	0.187481
Observations	88

ANOVA

	df	SS	MS	F	Significance F
Regression	4	5.10023	1.275058	36.27569527	1.6484E-17
Residual	83	2.917374	0.035149		
Total	87	8.017605			

	Coefficients	Standard Err	t Stat	P-value	Lower 95%	Upper 95%
Intercept	4.74538	0.092691	51.19546	1.44988E-64	4.561020746	4.929739823
bdrms	0.008321	0.029793	0.279305	0.780705385	-0.050936167	0.067578989
lotsize	5.65E-06	2.01E-06	2.807888	0.006214525	1.64785E-06	9.65225E-06
sqrft	0.000373	4.18E-05	8.926107	9.17915E-14	0.000289719	0.000455851
colonial	0.081465	0.045831	1.77752	0.079145776	-0.009690463	0.172620656

With the change in model, it now changes the interpretation of the coefficients.

$\beta_1 * 100$ is the percent change in home price for each additional bedroom, all else held constant. Thus, for each additional bedroom we anticipate the price of the home increasing by 0.8%. Notice that the only difference is that we use percent change on the variable that has the natural log.

$\beta_2 * 100$ is the percent change in home price for a unit change in lot size, all else held constant. Thus, for each additional square foot we anticipate the price of the home increasing by 0.03%.

Jumping ahead,

β_4 is the percent difference in home price of colonial homes compared to non-colonial homes all else held constant. Thus, if a home is a colonial home we anticipate the price of the home increasing by 8.1%. Remember that with categorical variables we interpret the coefficient as compared to the omitted benchmark. In this case the benchmark is simply "not a colonial home."

For some x-variables, it might be more intuitive to take the log of it. We can interpret these variables in a **"Log-Log" model** context. For example:

$$\ln(price) = \beta_0 + \beta_1(bedrooms) + \beta_2(\ln(lotsize)) + \beta_3(\ln(sqrft)) + \beta_4(colonial) + u$$

We didn't take the log of bedrooms, because intuitively we make unit changes of bedrooms. But for lot size, an increase in 1,000 square feet is a small change for a large lot and a big change for a small lot. Therefore, it might make sense to take the units out of it.

β_2 is the percent change in home price for a percent change in lot size, all else held constant. Again, we add percent into the interpretation on variables that have been logged. In this case, it is both on the price and the lot size.

β_3 is the percent change in home price for a percent change in the square footage of the home, all else held constant.

Some solid advice, do not take logs of dummy variables. It would be like, increasing the colonialness of the home by 1 percent would have a percent change on the home price. While technically that probably is possible if it is performed in an extremely convoluted fashion, please don't do it.

When should we take logs and when should we take a unit? Let's say we are both big shot mergers and acquisitions bankers and you make \$312,000 / year and I make \$310,000 / year. How upset would I be if I found out you made an extra \$2,000? Not very. That is a very small percentage and so much of our compensation is made up of bonuses. However, if we are both working a part-time job during university and you make \$12,000 / year and I make \$10,000 / year for the same work and performance, I could be pretty upset. In some scenarios percentages make much more sense in predicting an outcome than just the base unit.

It is important for us to note that the coefficients in our model may be incorrect because we do not have all of the necessary variables of a model included. This can bias some of our coefficients. The easiest way to capture this concept is with a simple example. Let's return to the hprice1.xlsx data set and run the following regression:

$$price = \beta_0 + \beta_1(bedrooms) + u$$

When we run this regression we see that the coefficient on bedrooms is 62.025. Or rather, for each additional bedroom we expect the price of a home to increase by $62,025. Let's suppose I'm constructing a 2,000 square foot home. How many bedrooms should I add? According to this model, why should I not construct the 2,000 square foot home with 10 bedrooms? The p-value on bedroom is also extraordinarily small. Those 10 bedrooms are definitely going to earn me an additional $620,246, right? What is wrong with this reasoning?

You might correctly point out that we are missing some very important information in our model. Namely, we do not have the square footage taken into account. Now run the following regression:

$$price = \beta_0 + \beta_1(bedrooms) + \beta_2(sqrft) + u$$

The coefficient on bedroom has fallen to 15.198, or $15,198 per bedroom. It is also no longer statistically significant at the 0.05 level. However, the square footage variable now tells us that for each additional square foot the price of the home increases by $128.

What just happened here? The bedroom variable was smuggling in it the effect of square footage. Number of bedrooms positively correlate with square footage, and square footage also correlates with home price. The end result is that the coefficient on bedrooms when square footage is omitted is too high. The coefficient on bedrooms is biased and is too high in our original regression.

A simplified form of how we can know the direction of omitted variable bias is the omitted variable bias triangle. First, we take the sign of the correlation (positive or negative) of X (the included variable) and Z (the omitted variable). We then multiply this number by the correlation between Z (the omitted variable) and Y (the dependent variable). The resulting sign tells you whether the coefficient is too high or too low.

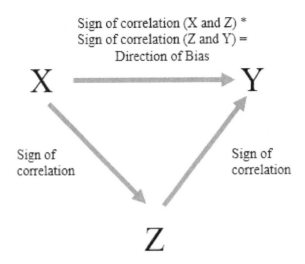

Let's walk through our example with bedrooms and square footage. The relationship between bedrooms and square footage is positive. As the number of bedrooms increases the number of square footage tends to increase. The relationship between square footage and price is positive. As the square footage increases the price of the home tends to increase. A positive number times a positive number is a … positive number. Thus, running the regression equation with square footage omitted results in a coefficient on bedrooms that is too high. When square footage is included we expect the coefficient on bedrooms to fall.

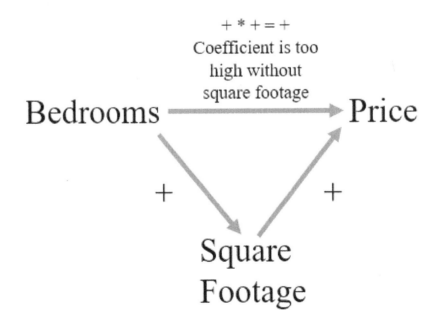

Chapter 6.7 Application: Model to Predict Home Prices

Use the data "home prices.xlsx" for the following example.
1. Write down your model that you would use to predict home prices
2. Run your model.
3. Interpret each coefficient in your model
4. How good is your model at predicting home prices?

Your Answer may be very different, but this is an example of how you might answer this question.

1. Model:

$$\ln(price) = \beta_0 + \beta_1(age) + \beta_2(rooms) + \beta_3(bathrooms) + \beta_4(\ln\_area) + \beta_5(\ln\_land)$$
$$+ \beta_6(year\ 1981) + \beta_7(nbh1) + \beta_8(nbh2) + \beta_9(nbh3) + \beta_{10}(nbh4)$$
$$+ \beta_{11}(nbh5) + \beta_{12}(nbh6) + u$$

It is important to note that (year 1981) is a dummy variable that equals one if the home was sold in 1981 and 0 if not. As there are 7 neighborhoods, a dummy variable is created for each variable except for nbh=0 because that is the omitted category. Also, notice that area and land have been transformed using the log function.

2. Below is our regression output.

SUMMARY OUTPUT

Regression Statistics	
Multiple R	0.886049
R Square	0.785082
Adjusted R Square	0.776709
Standard Error	0.207053
Observations	321

ANOVA

	df	SS	MS	F	Significance F
Regression	12	48.23459	4.019549	93.75884	3.53669E-95
Residual	308	13.20431	0.042871		
Total	320	61.43891			

	Coefficients	Standard Err	t Stat	P-value	Lower 95%	Upper 95%
Intercept	7.065232	0.39922	17.69758	7.64E-49	6.279688089	7.85077615
age	-0.00239	0.000419	-5.71331	2.61E-08	-0.003217442	-0.001568974
rooms	0.056086	0.017258	3.249763	0.001283	0.022126425	0.090045006
baths	0.144221	0.026138	5.517725	7.29E-08	0.092789652	0.195651803
larea	0.323799	0.052806	6.131806	2.66E-09	0.219891874	0.427705941
lland	0.104261	0.023729	4.393803	1.53E-05	0.057569185	0.15095225
y81	0.379796	0.024267	15.65091	4.96E-41	0.332046259	0.427545188
nbh1	-0.08679	0.047291	-1.83529	0.067426	-0.179848053	0.006261427
nbh2	-0.08402	0.038347	-2.19115	0.02919	-0.159477406	-0.008568719
nbh3	-0.21976	0.082482	-2.66438	0.008119	-0.382062685	-0.05746357
nbh4	-0.05851	0.041855	-1.39779	0.163181	-0.140863559	0.023853397
nbh5	-0.11623	0.046813	-2.48293	0.013563	-0.208345429	-0.024119615
nbh6	-0.07771	0.04347	-1.78759	0.074826	-0.163241479	0.00782931

3. Interpretation

β_0 is the average home price (in log points) of a home with all the variables set equal to zero. This number by itself is not feasible in this example.

$\beta_1 * 100$ is the percent change in home price for each change in the age of the home, all else held constant. That is making the home older by one year leads to a 0.2% estimated decrease in the home price.

$\beta_2 * 100$ is the percent change in the price for each additional room all else held constant. That is, for each additional room the price of the home is expected to increase by 5.6%.

$\beta_3 * 100$ is the percent change in the price for each additional bathroom, all else held constant. That is, one additional bathroom increasing the estimated price of the home increases by 14.4%.

β_4 is the percent change in the price for a percent change in the area or size of the home, all else held constant. That is, for each additional one percent increase in the square footage the estimated price of the home increases by .32%.

β_5 is the percent change in the price for a percent change in the land or lot size of the home, all else held constant. That is, for each additional one percent increase in the lot size the estimate price of the home increases by 0.1%

$\beta_6 * 100$ is the percent change in home price of homes in 1981 compared to 1978, all else held constant. That is, if a home is sold in 1981 rather than 1978, the estimated price of the home increases by 38%.

$\beta_7 * 100$ is the percent change in home price of a home in neighborhood 1 compared to homes in neighborhood 0, all else held constant. That is, if a home is located in neighborhood 1 rather than neighborhood 0, we estimate the price of the home to decrease by 8.7%.

$\beta_8 * 100$ is the percent change in home price of a home in neighborhood 2 compared to homes in neighborhood 0, all else held constant. That is, if a home is located in neighborhood 2 rather than neighborhood 0, we estimate the price of the home to decrease by 8.4%.

$\beta_9 * 100$ is the percent change in home price of a home in neighborhood 3 compared to homes in neighborhood 0, all else held constant. That is, if a home is located in neighborhood 3 rather than neighborhood 0, we estimate the price of the home to decrease by 22.0%.

$\beta_{10} * 100$ is the percent change in home price of a home in neighborhood 4 compared to homes in neighborhood 0, all else held constant. That is, if a home is located in neighborhood 4 rather than neighborhood 0, we estimate the price of the home to decrease by 5.9%.

$\beta_{11} * 100$ is the percent change in home price of a home in neighborhood 5 compared to homes in neighborhood 0, all else held constant. That is, if a home is located in neighborhood 5 rather than neighborhood 0, we estimate the price of the home to decrease by 11.6%.

$\beta_{12} * 100$ is the percent change in home price of a home in neighborhood 6 compared to homes in neighborhood 0, all else held constant. That is, if a home is located in neighborhood 6 rather than neighborhood 0, we estimate the price of the home to decrease by 7.7%.

4. How good is my model?

Let's start with R-squared. This tells me that my model describes 78.5 percent of the variation in home prices. That is more than before, but there is still about a quarter of the variation in home prices that we are not describing with our model. I would argue it is better than before, but if I made my living predicting home prices I would want to develop a better model (controlling for more factors) to increase the R-squared.

In spite of that, there are some important conclusions that I can draw from the model.

1. If I were to renovate my own, each bedroom I add would increase the price by 5.6 percent (this is statistically significant). Also, adding an additional bathroom would increase the price of the home by 14.4 percent (also statistically significant). Both of these are while controlling for the size of the home.
2. Increase the size of the home and the lot also increase the value of the home.
3. Homes increased in value from 1978 to 1981 by an average of 38 percent. That is a great growth rate. I should have bought a home in 1978 and then sold it in 1981.
4. All neighborhoods appear to have lower home prices than neighborhood 0. Neighborhoods 1 and 2 are significant at the 10 percent level and 3-5 are significant at the 5 percent level. There is no statistically significant difference in home values between neighborhood 6 and 0.

Made in the USA
Coppell, TX
12 September 2020